Introduction

Most people who like animals at all have a particular fondness for the babies. Whether it is a fluffy day-old chick, a cuddly-looking baby lion or a wide-eyed kangaroo joey peeping from its mother's pouch, a young animal seldom fails to fascinate. Although both young and full-grown animals are marvellous to behold, beyond their obvious appeal lies the serious business of survival in a generally hostile world . . . a struggle that is so vividly illustrated by a look into the lives of the babies.

In the wild, even baby carnivores have their problems. Although predators are few, many nonetheless become another creature's meal, while others die of disease or starvation and some fall prey to human hunters. Smaller mammals—like rodents—have such short lives and face so many dangers that, for the species to survive at all requires almost continuous breeding from a very early age. Of course, to protect their young many animals prepare a safe sheltered home where the babies remain until they can fend for themselves. Other babies, though, never know a home at all. Many animals—from zebras on the plains to whales in the ocean—are born ready to move into a nomadic way of life; while some—like the turtles that hatch from eggs left in the sand, or cuckoos that hatch in a 'host' nest—are simply deserted by their parents even before they are born.

Only rarely in the animal world do the babies have the benefit of both parents to care for them when they are at their most vulnerable. In many cases, the adult females and males only come together to mate, and then they separate before the babies are born. The mother usually takes over all the parental responsibilities, although—and nature has few rules without exceptions—these duties are sometimes fulfilled by the male alone. However, there are innumerable variations on the themes of reproduction and rearing of baby animals. Each is a marvel in itself, because every

animal is of course unique, and each species has evolved and adapted to its own particular circumstances.

Nowadays, though, humans have come to play a major part in the survival or extinction of every species of animal. Whereas once it was only hunting and fishing societies that threatened the animals directly, the human population explosion now makes almost every creature or its habitat a source of nourishment or wealth. This threat falls most heavily on the baby animals: if the adults are destroyed after they have bred then the species can survive, but to slaughter the young is to destroy altogether the possibility of breeding.

So, to understand more fully the workings of the natural world, a study of the babies is clearly an enlightening place to start. In the following pages of words and colour pictures, it is only possible to glimpse briefly into the lives of a few baby animals. Nonetheless, the extent of parental devotion or indifference, the levels of instinct and learning, the camouflage and survival techniques revealed, together surely add to our appreciation of the wonder of birth and the complexities of rearing.

Left: Although he is only three weeks old, this Tiger cub is already regarding the world with a wary eye. Right: Young Wart Hogs and their mother drinking at an African water hole.

Feathered babies

Birds—of enormously varying types—have lived on Earth ever since prehistoric times when their ancestors, who belonged to the reptile class, first took to the air. These creatures took such forms as the Pteranodon, the Pterodactyl and the famous Archaeopteryx, which is the oldest known bird. It had feathers on its body to replace the characteristic scales of reptiles, a long tail and a formidably toothed beak. From studies of fossils it has been found that the Archaeopteryx had at last made the step which would eventually lead to the 8,600 different species of bird we know today. Most birds still have scaly feet and a dinosaur-like skeleton, but most important of all— just like their cold-blooded ancestors and most of today's reptiles—birds lay eggs as part of their reproductive process. Unlike reptiles, however, birds are warm-blooded.

To hatch successfully, a fertilized egg must be incubated at a constant temperature; too high a temperature and the egg will cook; too cold and it will chill and the baby bird will never develop. To keep their eggs at the right temperature most birds brood on them. The transfer of heat from the parent bird's body to the eggs is helped by a featherless 'brood patch' produced hormonally on the bird's underside.

Not all birds, however, have brood patches and spend weeks or months sitting on their eggs. For example, King and Emperor Penguins shuffle around with their single egg on their feet and incubate it under a fold of skin which hangs from the lower abdomen. The gannets are another species that do not develop brood patches; their eggs are kept at a constant heat by their highly vascular feet. The Australian Brush Turkey and the Incubator Bird of the Philippines, meanwhile, have found an even easier method of incubation: they simply build a mound of leaves, earth and twigs (which can be as much as 3 m (9 ft) high and 6 m (18 ft) across) and then bury their eggs 1 m (3 ft) deep in this compost heap. The heat of the sun com-

bined with that of the rotting vegetation then does the job of incubation. A variation on this theme is used by the Great-headed Maleos which live on Sulawesi (formerly Celebes). These birds dig a deep hole in the black volcanic sand that covers areas of their mountainous island homes, deposit their eggs, and then cover them with the sand to keep them warm. In all these cases it is the male bird's job to maintain the correct temperature inside the mound by removing and replacing compost or sand as and when necessary.

In general, however, when the breeding season arrives most birds respond by building, borrowing or burrowing a structure of some kind in which to lay their eggs, keep them warm and safe, and then rear their babies until they are ready to start lives of their own.

Nests come in all shapes and sizes. Many birds weave elaborate homes from grass, moss, twigs and other suitable available materials; others casually wedge a few twigs in the fork of a tree. Some even squat in a ready-made home, occasionally forcing the previous occupant out, while other birds live communally or simply lay their eggs in a hollow in the ground. In fact, just as humans all over the world build homes in thousands of different ways, so the nests of the world's birds vary widely from species to species and place to place.

Finches: Apart from their absence from Madagascar and Antarctica, finches are among the world's most commonly seen birds. There are well over 100 species altogether and many of them, the Canary for instance, are renowned for their beautiful songs. Finches are small birds that exist primarily on a diet of seeds, buds and berries—their strong cone-shaped beaks are perfectly adapted to cope with these foods. However, there are exceptions that include insects in their diets, and insects are fed to the young.

The majority of finches live, and build their nests, in trees. The male and female birds form into pairs at the beginning of the breeding season, isolating themselves from other finches. The female builds a nest which is nearly always saucer shaped, but once again there are variations between the species. The

Left: Safe in their grass-lined mud nest under the eaves of a barn roof, these young swallows hungrily await the insects their mother has caught on the wing.

9

Left: This soft, fluffy duckling—a fledgling Mallard—is 'imprinted' with an image of its mother within a few hours of hatching although it already knows her voice, and has replied to it, from inside the egg. Soon after her brood has hatched, the mother will lead her tiny chicks in a wobbly line down to the water's edge ready for their first swim.
Right: A stork mother with her babies in the big untidy nest which is home for the first two months of their lives. Both parents feed their young by regurgitating food on to the edge of the nest and leaving the babies to scramble for the pieces. In this photograph the contrast between the orange beak of the adult Stork and the black beaks of the young birds can be seen clearly.

hen lays 4–6 eggs in the nest and then settles down to do most of the brooding. Incubation usually takes about 14 days and the male feeds the female during this time. When the baby finches are hatched, they are fed by both parents who catch insects and bring them back to the nest. Baby finches are born in a 'precocial' state, that is, their eyes are open and they are covered with fine down. They are able to move around and leave the nest within a few hours of hatching. Depending on the amount of food available during the breeding season, a pair of finches may rear as many as three broods of chicks.

Warblers: Most of the 300 species of warbler spend their lives on the African continent, a few are found in North America, and the rest are spread out over Europe, Asia and Australia. Warblers are not particularly good fliers (their wings are rather short) and they are clumsy and awkward on the ground, so they are usually seen creeping around reeds or bushes. The majority of warblers live solely on an insect diet although those species inhabiting northern latitudes also eat berries, especially in winter.

Warblers have been divided into two main biological groups: Reed-warblers and Bush- or Leaf-warblers. Many warblers of different species build very different kinds of nests, and some of them exhibit a wide range of interesting and unusual features. Garden Warblers and Blackcaps, for example, build cup-shaped nests made mainly of dried grasses, while Wood Warblers, Willow Warblers, Arctic Warblers and Chiffchaffs build spherical nests with a side opening. Cylindrical nests are typical of Reed Warblers, Sedge Warblers and Fan-tailed Warblers, while the Tailor Birds have a fascinating variation on this theme: they use their sharp, needle-like beaks to pierce holes in leaves and 'sew' them together with

plantwool or cobweb filaments and then make a nest of dried grass and plant fibre inside this sack. Whichever the species, however, once the hen warbler has made her nest and laid 3–5 eggs, both parents take turns at brooding. After 10–12 days the chicks hatch. They are 'altricial' at birth (that is, helpless and blind, with no down feathers or fat reserves) and stay in the nest until fully feathered. Their parents feed them with crushed insects and generally care for them until they are old enough to fly away and begin independent lives of their own.

Cuckoos: Although small birds like warblers are one of the cuckoo's choices of unwitting 'host', not all cuckoos are parasites that lay their eggs in the nests of other birds. In fact, the majority of the 130 species of true cuckoos build their own nests and rear their own young. One species, the American Anis, even builds communal nests of sticks, in which all the hens lay their eggs and share the duties of incubation and rearing. These are found in South America and can often be seen perching on cattle and feeding off their ticks, or running along the ground in search of insects and larvae. Other non-parasitic cuckoos include the North American Yellow-billed and Black-billed varieties, and the mainly ground-living Roadrunners (or Chaparral Cocks) which live in Asia and drier parts of North America; the Couas of Madagascar, and the Coucals found in Africa, southern Asia and Australia. These fast-moving birds, which fly badly, feed on reptiles, snakes and insects, build their own nests and care for their own babies.

On the other hand, the 47 species of cuckoo which are social parasites have to take certain precautions to ensure their baby's survival in the foster-parent's nest. Firstly, the cuckoo's egg must look roughly the same as the host's, and both must have similar

fledglings, even though they may be lying only a few inches from the nest. Also, a few birds just passing the nest might be lured by its incessant cries into feeding the cuckoo chick with insects intended for their own young. With all this food the chick grows rapidly and before it is ready to leave the nest after about a month it may have become twice the size of its foster parents. Needless to say, the baby cuckoo's real mother takes no interest in the incubation, hatching or rearing of her offspring. As a result, the cuckoo's distinctive vocal repertoire—which is completely unlike that of its foster parents—is thought to be genetically fixed, as the parasitic young have no opportunity to learn the song from other members of their species.

Varieties of cuckoo are widely distributed over Europe and the temperate and sub-tropical parts of Africa, America and Asia. Many which breed in the north fly south to spend the winter in tropical Africa. Others, like the Great-spotted Cuckoo, breed in Africa and southern Europe and often lay their egg in the nests of crows and rooks. The attractive Bronzed Cuckoo breeds on islands off New Zealand and specializes in laying its eggs in the nests of fly-catchers. When it is only a month old the young of this species sets out on an amazing journey: it flies 2000km (1240 miles) to Australia in pursuit of the adult Bronzed Cuckoos, and then heads north for another 1,600km (990 miles) to the Bismarck and Solomon Islands.

Goslings: Unlike cuckoos, geese are firmly united in family groups, and male and female pairs often remain together for many years or even their whole lives. They lay their eggs in nests assembled on the ground, and within a few hours of hatching the fluffy, down-covered goslings are able to follow their parents, although it is another two months before their flight feathers are sufficiently developed for them to take to the air.

Around the world—but especially in the northern hemisphere—there are many different varieties of geese, and they are often found together in huge flocks. Many types have been domesticated for centuries both in Europe and the Far East, but the largest and perhaps the best-known of all—and the ancestor of our domesticated fowl—is the Greylag.

This bird breeds in Iceland, northern Europe and central Asia, and can be distinguished from other varieties by its short bill and heavy head. It likes to build a large nest lined with down, usually in marshes or lakeside rushes, close to a plentiful supply of its staple food, grass. Four, five or six large white eggs (although sometimes as many as eight or nine) are laid at the end of March, and the mother Greylag then broods on them for 27–29 days. Unlike many birds, geese have the ability to retrieve an egg and return it to the nest if it should fall out. Meanwhile,

incubation periods. Then, when the single cuckoo egg has been hatched, the host bird must be one which will be sure to provide the baby cuckoo with a supply of suitable food. In order to stimulate the foster-parents into giving it more food than their own chicks, the young cuckoo must also be able to beg with the right sort of signals. Not surprisingly, then, the hen Common Cuckoo does not just make a random choice of hosts with whom to leave her four to five eggs each year. The nests she chooses usually belong to small, insect-eating birds like Wrens, Robins, Reed or Willow Warblers or Meadow Pipits. If the adult host bird generally eats fruit and seeds, for example, then it has to be a bird which feeds its young on insects. As a final precaution, when the hen cuckoo lays her egg in a nest, she removes one of the host bird's eggs and consequently the total number of eggs remains the same.

Once the baby cuckoo has hatched, even though it is blind, feeble and naked, it soon gets rid of the competition by pushing any other eggs, or fledglings out of the nest until it is the only occupant. The foster parents, with their instinctive urge to feed chicks, are so stimulated by the baby cuckoo's gaping mouth and begging calls for food that they will make absolutely no effort to help their own starving

claws and a strong hind toe, as well as webbed feet, they are able to cling easily to tree branches. One perching duck species of interest is the Mandarin Duck found in East Asia. For hundreds of years this bird has been a Chinese symbol of conjugal fidelity, because of the devotion a pair show to each other.

Ducks which live on water and feed on snails, larvae and aquatic plants are divided into two groups: the dabbling ducks and the diving ducks.

Dabblers are so called because they feed by dipping their bills, heads and necks underwater to hunt for food. Among the most common variety is the Mallard or Wild Duck, the ancestor of the domestic ducks found in farmyards. Along with other dabblers like Teals, Pintails and Shovelers, Mallards are also favoured as 'game' birds.

Except for the summertime, when his brilliant plumage is in eclipse and he resembles the female, the Mallard drake's neck and head are a brilliant glossy green, his wings are brown with a violet-blue speculum, bordered with black and two white bars. The rest of his body is greyish white, his beak is greenish yellow and his feet are a bright orange-red.

Mallard parents form lasting relationships in October, well before the breeding time, and then spend the winter together. From February onwards the pairs head towards their breeding territory. They nest wherever there is enough food, but prefer to be on the banks of lakes, marshes or ponds. The actual site of the nest is chosen by the drake. Buildings, hollow trees, and even the old nests of crows or birds of prey have been found in use. The mother Mallard gathers together plants and grasses and builds the cup-shaped nest herself, finally lining it with down and feathers. Between the end of February and the beginning of May she will lay one pale-green egg each day, usually no more than 14 and no less than 7. Until she has finished laying, she camouflages the nest and covers the eggs with grass every day. When she has laid all her eggs she starts to brood, but makes sure that the nest is concealed with down every time she leaves it. The ducklings hatch after 28 days of incubation, and once they are dry she calls them down to the water. They are natural swimmers, and are soon hunting for food.

Like other birds, ducklings are imprinted with the characteristics of their 'mother'. For example, if the real mother is removed soon after hatching and is replaced by a substitute making the right sort of noises, the ducklings will grow up preferring the characteristics and companionship of this 'parent'.

Within a few days, as the ducklings develop, they

Above left: These altricial Blackbird chicks' yellow-lined, gaping mouths constantly stimulate their hard-working mother to feed them. Left: Fluffy Sparrowhawk fledglings seem to be threatening rather than begging for their ration of freshly killed meat.

become covered with brown feathers. They are able to fly by the time they are two months old, although many have by then succumbed to predators.

The other main group of aquatic ducks, known as the diving ducks, are different in many respects from the dabblers. Whereas dabblers feed at, or just below, surface level, pochards dive to get grass and mollusc food from the bed. These birds are heavy and thick set and are not so popular with human hunters. Pochards prefer clear, open water for most of the time, but during the nesting season they switch to the reeds and marsh vegetation. When feeding however, they can often be seen to disappear completely underwater for a few moments, before bobbing up to the surface again at almost the same spot. Diving ducks have great difficulty walking on dry land, because their legs are very wide apart and set far back on their bodies. Their feet, which are webbed across three toes, only add to their walking problems.

Like geese, diving ducks are found all over the world, although they are also concentrated in the northern hemisphere. They seem to prefer mostly colder or continental areas, and the Eider Duck, for instance, lives on the shores of countries stretching from Ireland's Atlantic coast to Estonia on the Baltic Sea. In many places Eider Ducks are semi-domesticated, and the down collected from nesting boxes is prized as a duvet filling. The Canvasback, the Tufted Duck, the Scaup, the Common Pochard and the Red-crested Pochards are other well-known diving ducks.

The Red-crested Pochard species usually contains more drakes than hens, this sexual imbalance being most noticeable at the start of the breeding season when the drakes are in pursuit of a mate. Amorous males often chase females through the air, putting on a spectacular flying display at the same time. As the breeding season gets further underway, the hens choose mates and begin to build their nests from green or dry leaves, stalks, roots or other available materials. When it is built the nest looks like a cone with the tip chopped off, and is sited on reeds or mud close to shallow water. The top of the nest is a deep cup with a lining of soft materials. The 6–10 creamy-coloured eggs, laid between April and May, sit in this cup surrounded by down. If there is a shortage of nesting space, several hens have been known to share one large nest, filling it with up to 32 eggs. Usually, though, the hen broods on her own eggs (which can sometimes be heard cheeping in response to a sound or movement from the mother) while the drake stands guard close by. If danger approaches, he warns his mate by taking flight. She calmly does the same, first swimming a little way from her nest. If unattached males begin to molest the brooding female, the drake will drive them away.

About four weeks after they are laid, the eggs hatch

Left: This untidy-looking chick may seem little more than a wide-eyed, downy baby at first glance, but within a few months it will have grown into an Eagle Owl, one of the most fearsome of the birds of prey. The species is the largest of the European owls, but is also found in Asia and Africa. Fully-grown adults have a pair of black horn-like tufts of feathers growing out of their heads, and may reach over 0·6m (2ft) in length with a wing-span of almost 1·8m (6ft). Eagle Owls live in remote, wooded areas and usually build their sparse nests of dead leaves among rocks. Two or three white eggs are laid each year and both parents share in feeding the chicks. All manner of small mammals and birds are taken by the birds during their twilight hunting forays, and even roe deer have been known to fall victim to their powerful talons and sharp, hooked beaks.
Right: A young Tawny Owl perches on a branch waiting to be fed. These are nocturnal birds of prey, particularly well known throughout Europe, western Asia, and north-west Africa for their distinctive 'hooting' call.

revealing tiny ducklings covered with fluffy down which is dark olive-brown with pale yellow spots on the upper parts, and pale on the underside. Within a few hours of hatching, the mother duck leads the babies from the nest to the nearest water and there they very quickly learn to feed on insects and plants. If an enemy approaches, the mother duck will flap away from her ducklings with fluttering movements that give the appearance of an injured or sick bird trying desperately to get into the air and fly away. At this signal from their mother, the babies will immediately dive and swim underwater, come up for air when necessary, then dive and swim again until they are out of the danger zone. The mother duck—having focused the enemy's attention on herself and averted the threat to her chicks—then takes to the air.

Like all other aquatic birds, ducks have a useful gland called the oil, or preen, gland over the root of the tail. The waxy secretion from this gland is applied to the feathers with the beak at frequent intervals, and this preening helps to make the bird's plumage water-proof. If an aquatic bird is unable to oil its feathers, it may develop pneumonia, or become waterlogged and drown.

Storks: Some of the most distinctive birds found near water are those known as the wading birds. Storks belong to this family which also includes Spoonbills, Flamingos, Bitterns, Shoebills and Hammerheads. Wading birds have long featherless legs and four webbed toes on each foot. Their beaks are long with sharp cutting edges and they mostly eat amphibians and fish. They are all strong fliers.

The most popular of the 17 species of stork is the very sociable White Stork, which is almost domestic-ated in parts of Scandinavia and several northern European countries. Regarded as auspicious by many, White Storks are often found nesting on such high, obvious sites as tree tops, church towers, roofs and chimney stacks. Every year the same pair arrive at their old nest, rebuilding it at the start of each breeding season. As the years go by, the nest may become massive—some have weighed over 50 kg (110 lb).

The eggs are laid between the end of April and the beginning of May and, after 30 days' incubating by both parents, three to five baby storks hatch in a precocial state. Unlike their silent parents baby storks are very noisy, constantly whistling, croaking and whining for food. Water is regurgitated directly into their throats, but all food is placed at the edge of the nest and the babies reach out for it.

By the time they are eight days old, the baby storks have their second coat of down. Flying lessons begin at two months, and a month after they have learned to fly properly, the baby White Storks join all the other storks for the long flight to Africa, where they stay until the end of the cold northern winter.

Birds of prey

Owlets: The 150 species of owl are similar enough to share many of the same characteristics. Nearly all are nocturnal birds of prey which hunt for mammals, reptiles and amphibians during the twilight hours; they all possess excellent hearing, and, because of the marvellous design of their wings, fly silently which gives them a tremendous advantage over their unsuspecting prey. However, nesting habits differ so greatly that owls have been divided into two families: true owls and barn (or screech) owls.

A true owl will lay her eggs in a hole in a tree, another bird's discarded nest, the underside of a rock, a crevice in a rock, in fact anywhere that will give sufficient shelter for her eggs. Barn owls, on the other hand, nest between rafters in lofts, barns, deserted houses, garden sheds and so on. They also return to the same nesting place every year.

True owls and barn owls do have more or less the same breeding habits, though. Wherever the eggs are laid they are incubated for between 32–35 days by the female. During this time, her food is provided by the male. Between two and six (depending on the species) altricial chicks hatch, and they are fed up to ten times a night with voles, mice, rabbits and other small mammals which are ripped into bite-sized morsels by the parents. After five days the chicks are able to see and in a few short weeks all their feathers have grown and they are able to fly. Meanwhile, during the time they spend in the nest, their parents are extremely protective towards them; they are capable of drawing blood from any intruder, even those many times their size.

Eagles, like Falcons, Sparrowhawks, Vultures and Buzzards are in no way related to owls. They are diurnal—not nocturnal—birds of prey. Various species are found in Asia, Africa, the Americas, Europe and Scandinavia. All varieties eat meat, although different species have diet preferences which range from snakes to monkeys, and carrion to voles. They use their marvellous eyesight to find food, then seize it with their sharp talons and carry it back to their eyrie, or nest. There it is ripped to pieces and eaten.

Eagles form lasting pairs for breeding and use the same remotely-sited eyrie from one year to the next. This collection of twigs and branches lined with bark and dried grass normally houses between one and three blind, naked and helpless eaglets by the middle of the year. However, only the fittest of these—usually the first to hatch—will normally survive, having starved the others by eating all the food or killing them outright. Eaglets grow quickly on the meat provided by the parents, and by the time they are three months old they can fend for themselves, having already been taught to fly. However, an eaglet will not have its full adult plumage until its fifth year.

Sea birds

Many water birds live by the sea because their former inland habitats have been taken over by the 'progress' of human activities as diverse as river-polluting factories, marsh-drainage schemes and lakeside tourist resorts. For these birds the sea offers a rich food supply and wide open spaces denied them inland. Gulls, meanwhile, are among the bird world's most successful members. Although they are basically coastal birds, they roam happily far and wide in search of

Left: A Northern Gannet and its chick. When the fledgling's first set of all-white flight feathers develop, it is abandoned by its parents. Later, when it is adult, the young bird will itself get black wingtips like its parent in the photograph.
Right: Like Gannets, Kittiwakes breed in large colonies on coastal cliffs. However, these small gulls seem to prefer the narrowest, most inaccessible ledges on which to build their nests of seaweed and rear their chicks.

food, eating almost anything from human refuse to young chicks, eggs and small mammals.

Other birds, however, are exclusively maritime, never venturing inland except to breed. They spend the rest of their lives living, eating and sleeping on the seas and coastlines. These are the true sea birds.

Kittiwakes: Similar to the Common Gull in size and appearance, Kittiwakes inhabit the North Atlantic, and are distinguishable by their black wing tips. They live on the sea for many months at a time, feeding on a diet of fish supplemented by plankton, insects and molluscs. They only come ashore for the breeding season which begins in February, and then thousands of these normally silent birds form noisy colonies on steep cliff-faces. Pairs form on the site and bowl-shaped nests are constructed by both the male and the female out of seaweed and sea grasses. The nest is lined with dry grass on a sturdy base of moss, grass and mud. Nests are often placed right next to each other, and they are well protected by their practically inaccessible locations. After 28 days of incubation, two baby Kittiwakes are hatched and, unlike most other sea-bird chicks, they are altricial at birth. This unusual state—and their clawed toes—appear to be precautions related to the normally precarious position of the nest. As a result, they have to remain as still as possible and hang on to avoid falling out. To feed, the chicks thrust their tiny beaks down the parent's throat and grab food. They grow quickly and learn to fly in about six weeks, although they will not be fully mature for another three years.

Gannets: Unless they are nesting, Gannets also spend their lives on the high seas fishing in large flocks. They catch and swallow their fish underwater, and have special 'shock-absorber' air sacks under the skin to reduce the impact of dives 5 m (16 ft) under

the water from as high as 30 m (100 ft) above the surface.

During the breeding season, these large birds gather in thousands on sheer rocky coasts of the North Atlantic from the Channel Islands to Newfoundland. Pairs form and the couple heap together seaweed, debris and plants to make a circular nest in which one egg is laid. Both adults take their turn at incubation, and since they do not develop brood patches the egg is incubated between their blood-warmed feet.

After 44 days the chick is born blind, naked, helpless and with a great appetite for regurgitated fish which it takes from its parents' throats. Its first dark feathers appear when it is six weeks old; at 11 weeks it is effectively abandoned by its parents when they stop feeding it. After it has starved for a few days and lost some weight the chick heads out to sea, where it teaches itself to fish and dive. From then on, it becomes whiter after each year's moult and attains its full dazzling-white adult plumage only after five years.

Terns: The most widely-distributed species of tern is the Common Tern which breeds on beaches in Europe, North America and the cooler parts of western Asia. Other species include the Black Tern, the Whiskered Tern, the Caspian Tern, the Arctic Tern and the Little Tern; together they are often known as sea-swallows because of their forked tails and agile flight.

The Common Tern is a ground-nester, and lays two or three eggs on clumps of grass, plant stems or gravel. Colonies of them can number up to 10,000 birds. The mother broods on the eggs and is fed by the father for around 22 days until the chicks hatch. As soon as their down is dry the young leave the nest to search for shade from the hot sun, as the sand and shingle get too hot for them. They come back to the

nest only when they are hungry, but in between many are lost to predators such as rats, crows and gulls. At the first hint of danger the parents call and the chicks freeze where they are. However, the survival rate is only around 20 per cent. Terns have difficulty walking on land but once they are airborne they are marvellous fliers who catch fish by skimming along the sea surface and spearing them with their beaks. They are often seen in flocks intermingled with large numbers of skuas and gulls.

Albatrosses: These mysterious birds, which are close relatives of the petrels and shearwaters, are rarely seen on land. They normally live south of the equator, where open ocean covers most of the hemisphere. Traditionally, sailors regard a sighting of this swan-sized bird as a good omen—their wanderings across the oceans in search of food (their favourite being squid) sometimes brought them into contact with lonely ships at sea.

When the breeding instinct rises, albatrosses make for land and usually arrive under cover of darkness. They nest in colonies on remote Pacific islands; they do not build conventional nests but dig out a burrow or depression on the ground. Then they build a wall of earth around it and the mother lays one large egg inside. This egg usually takes about eight weeks to hatch, although the Royal Albatross's egg has the longest incubation time of any known bird as it can take up to 80 days before the chick emerges. Both parents brood on the egg and help to rear the chick; in the cases of the Royal and Wandering species the chick is not able to fly until it is nearly a year old. Consequently these particular species only breed every other year, although in other varieties the interval is shorter. Nonetheless, albatross chicks develop very slowly on their diet of predigested food, and will themselves not be able to breed until their eighth year.

Babies with hooves

The world's hoofed mammals are collectively known as 'ungulates', and two main groups are recognized: those with an odd number of toes (one or three), and those with an even number of toes (two or four).

Generally speaking, hoofed mammals—and especially their babies—are vulnerable to a wide range of ferocious, carnivorous predators. Accordingly, most of them live in herds or flocks which to an extent afford some protection from their enemies since, when it is threatened, the whole herd is able to move together to escape and only those individuals who are weak or ill are left behind to face the danger.

Although it would seem likely that mothers and their newly-born young are also very vulnerable, this is not the case at all. Female ungulates give birth while they are standing. This position is convenient because firstly they are able to spot any possible danger before it becomes a threat to them, and secondly most of the other herd members are also standing so the mother does not attract too much attention to herself. Compared to many other mammalian babies, ungulate babies are exceedingly well advanced at birth. They are able to see clearly and (depending on the species) are able to run with the herd or flock within a few minutes or hours of their birth. Apart from avoiding danger, the mother and baby have also to be able to keep up with the herd or flock when it moves on to fresh pastures. There is no problem about this when the baby is mobile immediately, or soon after, it is born.

Generally, most ungulates are able to run well. What look like their knees are actually their ankles, as the ankle bones have fused together and lengthened to provide maximum leverage and power for running.

Ponies, horses and donkeys

These odd-toed ungulates are closely related and all belong to the family Equidae. Asses and zebras also belong to this family. Members are able to cross-breed and babies are known as mules or hinnies.

Ponies: To qualify as ponies, small horses must not exceed $14\frac{1}{2}$ hands in height from the ground to the

Left: This long-legged, baby donkey is only a few days old. However it is already standing firm. The apparent urgency with which young hoofed quadrupeds struggle to their feet and start to move around after being born is a necessary survival measure in the wild where carnivorous predators would soon claim a baby, and its mother, if they become separated from the rest of their herd as it moved on in search of fresh grazing.

Right: A newborn pony is pictured here trying to raise itself for the first time. After being born, the pony will recover its strength and lie on the ground for several minutes before beginning the wobbly business of first raising its hind legs and then its front legs. Like the donkey, however, this young pony will be able to run around within its first few hours of life.

withers, that is, the ridge between the shoulder blades. Ponies are small because the herds live in harsh, inhospitable regions of the world, including mountainous, desert and heathland areas. The smallest breed in the world are the Shetland Ponies. They are bred on the Shetland Islands north of Scotland which are exposed to severe weather conditions. The soil is poor and stony and offers only sparse vegetation for food. In spite of these drawbacks, Shetland Ponies are strong and hardy. They live in herds, each led by a dominant male who keeps a watchful eye on them as they spend their days grazing on the available scanty vegetation.

Apart from the dominant male leaders, the herd is composed of many mares and their foals, the younger stallions having been driven out by the leader.

The male leader of the herd mates with all the mares and about 11 months later the ponies are born. After they are licked clean by their mothers, the babies rest for a while before tottering to their feet and going to their mothers' teats for the first feed of lactose-rich milk. Within a few hours, the babies are trotting along confidently next to their mothers.

Shetland Ponies are sometimes used for light draught work. They are also used in riding schools as riding ponies or are kept as pets for small children. They grow to a maximum height of 1m (39in).

Sometimes, pony breeds are crossed with horse breeds to meet human requirements for riding and improved stock. The Dale and Fell breeds, for instance, are often crossed with small Thoroughbred or Arab sires to produce foals which become riding ponies of an excellent quality; Welsh Ponies sometimes vary greatly in appearance as they have been crossed with English, Hackney and Arab blood; New Forest Ponies have also been 'improved' at various times with the introduction of blood from other breeds.

Horses: Every known breed of horse—with the exception of Przewalski's Horse—is domesticated, and different types have been intensively bred to perform specific tasks. Some breeds are used as racehorses, others for hunting; heavy horses have been developed for draught work, and so on. Nevertheless, the breeding pattern is the same for all types.

Mares and stallions are usually mated when both are about three years old. If there is no stallion available, the mare may be artificially inseminated.

Below: This picture of a pretty foal, sharp wire and a broken fence illustrates just how easily humans can, through carelessness, maim the animals they are proud to own.
Right: These two foals, like all children, enjoy playing together, and will no doubt soon be off in a spirited gallop down the paddock.

After a gestation period which lasts between 11 and 13 months, one foal is born. Its birth weight varies, depending on whether it is a heavy or light breed, and those foals born of heavy breeds weigh about 60kg (130lb), whereas the lighter foals weigh between 40–45kg (88–100lb). The foal is suckled by its mother and if the weather is favourable it is put in a field to graze with her. With the combination of milk and grass, it soon grows strong and healthy. If it is a male foal and it is not going to be used for breeding purposes, it is castrated any time after it is two months old and it is then known as a 'gelding'.

The baby shares the oats and bran put out for its mother until it is separated from her at the age of about six months. When it is about two years old, the filly (female) or colt (male) starts to undertake light tasks or can be raced. By the time it is three or four years old, the horse is mature enough to undertake adult tasks.

Przewalski's Horse, or the Mongolian Wild Horse, is the only surviving race of pure-bred wild horse in the world today. It is found in central Asia and there the mares and their young roam the open plains moving from one grazing ground to the next led by a single stallion, with other, less powerful males confined to the dangerous margins of the herd.

The dominant stallion serves most of the females

Above: Minutes after their birth, baby Peruvian llamas like this one are on their feet and bounding around.
Right: Mountain Goat kids are born with horn buds already showing and, like llamas, are also on their feet within minutes of being born.

during the spring. Almost exactly one year later the foals are born. The mothers stand to deliver their single babies which are licked clean when born and, as in all mammals except humans, the placenta is eaten. Although the baby is tired after its journey into the world, it rests for only a short while before standing and starting to suckle milk from its mother's teats. Within a few hours it is able to trot alongside its mother.

As the young foals grow older they play together, sometimes galloping around as fast as they can or rearing up in mock fights. As they grow up, however, their lives change. The young colts are not allowed to remain in the herd, for it already has one stallion, and so they are forced to the fringes where they wait until either they are able to start their own herd by abducting a few of the more willing mares, or they fall prey to a predator. The fillies are much more favoured by the herd's dominant stallions. As they do not represent a sexual threat to him, he allows them to stay and join his harem.

Donkeys: This African animal was first domesticated in Egypt, and its nearest relatives are the Wild African Asses which roam the semi-arid grasslands of Ethiopia and Somalia. Donkeys are placid, hardy creatures, well adapted to a hot dry climate and sensitive to cold weather. They are particularly useful for pack work as they do not need much food and can work much longer hours than a horse, even going up to 12 hours between meals.

One baby donkey is born after a 12-month gestation period—twins are a very rare occurence. Like all other ungulates, baby donkeys are able to run along-side their mothers within a few hours of their birth.

Mountain and desert babies
Llamas: These South American even-toed ungulates are very closely related to camels but do not have humps. The Guanaco and Vicuña are two wild species of llama, and both are found on the western coastal areas of South America.

Baby Guanacos are born into the most widespread species. The small herds—up to 10 females and their

babies led by a male—graze in the uplands at 5000m (16,400ft) during the rainy season. Guanacos are able to reach such heights because their blood is very efficient at absorbing oxygen. When the weather is dry, they come down to sea level.

During the rutting season, the male leader of the herd and the other males fight desperately for possession of the females. Eventually the babies are conceived and after a 10–11 month gestation period they are born from a standing position. The babies are very advanced and after they have been licked clean they are able to run around immediately. Although the baby llama only suckles from its mother until it is about three months old, maternal care and protection continues for another two months after it is weaned. Then, if it has the misfortune to be born male, the calf is driven from the herd by the dominant male and it is forced to join an exclusively male herd of dispossessed llamas. If, however, the baby is female, she is welcomed into the herd and will herself become pregnant the following year.

Wild sheep and goats: Baby Mouflons are even-toed ungulates and are born during the spring in the mountainous regions of Corsica and Sardinia. Each ewe, for Mouflons are European wild sheep, gives birth to up to three precocious lambs that are able to run around within minutes of being born. However, the herd (which is led by the oldest ewe) waits until nightfall before starting to move around and chew the cud, as all ruminants do.

As they get older the females and males develop in different ways: the rams grow long backwards-curving horns and pale, sharply-defined saddle areas on their sides which contrast markedly with their mainly rusty colour; the females, on the other hand, might grow short horns if any grow at all. When they are sexually mature after a year they pair in the autumn, and the next generation of Mouflon babies is born in the spring.

Like Mouflons, Mountain Goats are highland dwellers, although their homes are to be found in Asia Minor. Baby Mountain Goats are born in May or June when each mother has a single kid, which by the time it is half an hour old is nimbly climbing

Left: Camels are meant to be ugly, awkward, vicious and smelly 'ships of the desert', but it would be difficult to put such harsh words to the delightful Arabian baby seen here. Although its colour contrasts sharply with that of its companions, it is not at all unusual for baby camels, like llamas, to start life several shades paler than their parents. Also, at this stage young camels are able to show off two pairs of smooth legs. Later, the trials of being a domesticated load-carrier will produce large black callouses on both front and rear legs where the animals are taught to kneel.
Above right: This baby Bighorn or Rocky Mountain Sheep is nimble-footed very soon after birth and has soft foot pads to absorb the impact of jumping around on precipitous, rocky slopes.
Right: Only a few hours after its birth, this Mouflon lamb is already on its feet.

among the rocks and bushes on the craggy slopes at altitudes up to 4000m (13,000ft). The baby Mountain Goat is conceived during the winter and the gestation lasts for five months.

Bighorn Sheep are another breed whose babies are born on the most isolated and inaccessible mountains of North America and north-east Siberia. This breed are also called Rocky Mountain Sheep. Lambs are born into a herd containing about 50 ewes; the males often live solitary lives or have their own herd elsewhere.

Within a few minutes of birth, the young are nimbly leaping and bounding over the rocks. Their sure-footedness ensures that they are excellent climbers too. With their warm, shaggy white coats, the harsh cold and piercing winds present no problem to the lambs, and by the time they are mature they can weigh up to

135kg (300lb) and stand 1·2m (4ft) high at the shoulder. *Camels:* Many thousands of years ago, the camel family originated in North America. From there, the llama branch went to South America and the camels themselves migrated to Asia, becoming extinct in North America.

The wild Bactrian Camels of the Gobi Desert were thought to be extinct until a herd was sighted in 1957. However, these animals are closely related to the domesticated beasts of burden which are larger. Both have two humps of fatty tissue, one over the shoulder and the other over the hind-quarters, and they are massive creatures which stand 2m (6½ft) at the shoulder and are about the same length, although some do grow over 3·3m (11ft) long.

With a gestation lasting 350–400 days, it is just about possible for a female to give birth once a year.

Left: Both the Fallow fawn and the tiny baby Dikdik (above) can remain perfectly still and almost invisible in the undergrowth while their mothers are away foraging for food.

The baby's coat is lighter than that of its mother at birth and, like the other ungulates, it is born from a standing position and is soon strong enough to run with the herd.

The domesticated variety is a triple-purpose animal, used as a means of transport, a source of meat and leather and also as a supplier of milk. When their babies are born, they do not possess the characteristic callosities on their knees, breastbone and on all the joints which touch the ground when the animal is kneeling to be loaded or unloaded. These 'scars' are developed in the course of a working life and are not hereditary.

The domesticated Arabian or One-humped Camel (Dromedary) suckles her calf in the hot, sandy deserts of north Africa and central and south-west Asia. The baby is physically well-prepared for life in the desert, with long eyelashes to protect its eyes from the stinging sand, nostrils which can be closed, broad feet to prevent it from sinking into soft sand, reserves of fat stored in its hump and thick, leathery, tough lips that can cope with the most coarse and thorny desert vegetation. When the baby is weaned and is old enough to work it is employed as a pack animal, carrying loads of 130–180kg (300–400lb) on its back for distances of up to 65km (40 miles) every day across desert terrain, with only minimal needs of food and water.

Deer and antelope

The many species of deer and antelope are all members of the ruminant sub-order of even-toed ungulates, as are sheep and goats. Ruminants have a compound stomach with four compartments to the alimentary tract between the gullet and the intestine. The first compartment is the 'rumen' or 'paunch'. Animals which ruminate their food swallow the cropped grass or leaves before it is thoroughly chewed. This food passes into the rumen where the cellulose is broken down by bacterial fermentation. After this breakdown, the food passes into the honeycomb stomach where it is assembled into small pellets which are regurgitated back to the mouth and thoroughly masticated and ground to a pulp in the cud-chewing process. When this has happened, the food is again swallowed and passes back through the rumen, but is by-passed into the remaining three stomach compartments to be digested before excretion.

Roe Deer: The female Roe Deer gives birth to two young—generally a female and a male—nine months after the rutting season which occurs during July and August. They are born in a thicket and their coats are tawny, marked with three lines of white spots which disappear by the time they are a year old. Although the fawns can stand almost as soon as they are born, they remain hidden and wait for their mother to feed them. She does not bring them out into the open woods for about two weeks, and then they join their father and remain as a family group until the two young are driven away at the end of winter, by which time they are able to fend for themselves.

The young roebuck's antlers do not grow until he is well into his second year of life. At first his bony outgrowths are simply unbranched prongs covered with velvety skin. This skin soon dries and is rubbed off. Eventually the short antlers are shed in the middle of winter and then new ones start to grow. This time, though, they are forked, although they are once again shed in the winter. This process continues and full antler development does not occur until the roebuck is four years old. The doe, in contrast, is a smaller animal than the buck and does not develop antlers at all.

These timid creatures live in the woods of Britain,

Left: Even the full-grown Suni antelope of east and east-central Africa only stands 33–35cm (13–14 in) at the shoulder, so the really minuscule proportions of this young baby can easily be appreciated. Nonetheless, this tiny and vulnerable creature is extremely active from birth and is also born with acute senses so it stands a good chance of both detecting and evading predators, like large pythons.

Right: Like the Suni, the small Steinbuck antelope also has keen senses from birth to help detect the presence of predators. The large, moist nose, enormous moveable ears and wide eyes of this young baby are evidence enough of that. However, this one's mother takes no chances and after giving birth in long grass, she conceals her young in a hole in the ground for the first few days of its life while she is away grazing for food.

Europe and Asia as far east as China, feeding on foliage as well as eating fungi and berries.

Fallow Deer: Although Fallow Deer are native to Mediterranean countries, they also live as park animals in north European countries. In May or June, when the babies are born, all the females (or hinds) live together in exclusively female herds. Each normally gives birth to a single fawn, although two or even three are not unknown. From the first, the babies are well developed and can run soon after birth if they have to. They feed on their mother's milk and by the end of summer the females and their sturdy fawns join the male herd in time for the mating season which occurs in late October. The sexes separate at the end of winter, and the hinds and fawns spend more time together before the fawns leave.

Male Fallow Deer develop antlers and can breed at the age of three. The females, in contrast, do not develop antlers and can breed at the age of two.

Impalas: These antelopes live in herds which range from Kenya to South Africa. They are quite large animals and are famous for their impressive jumping ability. The babies are born after a six-month gestation period, and are very active and can stand and run with the herd only a few hours after birth. If it is threatened, the baby is able to leap 3m (10ft) into the air, or up to 10½m (35ft) in bounds to the nearest cover.

Dikdiks: This tiny antelope is about the size of a hare when it is fully grown. It has a long nose, huge eyes and a very short tail and a tuft of hair on the top of its head. Not much is known about baby Dikdiks, except that although they are tiny at birth, they are able to stand and walk within a short time. Like Impalas, they are also able to leap high into the air and bound away if they are frightened.

Babies in burrows and nests

Many different animals and birds choose burrows or nests for their homes. Some—like Genets, Hyenas and small Wild Cats—are anything but defenceless, and are in fact very aggressive carnivores. In general, however, animals choosing burrows or nests to live or breed in are by nature rather vulnerable. For them—the rats, mice, rabbits, hamsters, and so on—life presents an abundance of enemies.

A second common feature of these animals is that either individually or as a species they normally exhibit an outstanding ability to survive. The hedge-

Left: Small furry rodents like Long-tailed Field Mice and hamsters (below) represent a tasty snack to hundreds of predatory birds, mammals and reptiles, and so they have to reproduce on a grand scale to ensure the survival of the species.

hog's spines, the hare's speed and the rabbit's acute senses and labyrinthine warrens are clear examples of this. Also, most of these creatures ensure survival as a species by their amazing fertility which ensures reproduction on a grand scale. In ideal conditions, for instance, a single pair of rats could have around 20 million descendants in just three years!

Like rats, mice are rodents: they have to gnaw at things constantly to grind down their two pairs of persistently growing incisor teeth. They are extremely active little creatures, and have successfully adapted to life all around the world.

Wood Mice: In Europe and parts of Scandinavia, one of the most common mouse varieties is the Wood Mouse (also known as the Long-tailed Field Mouse). These creatures inhabit gardens, woods, fields and

35

hedgerows, and build their homes in burrows under roots or occasionally under heaps of rotting compost. When the breeding season begins in early spring a globe-shaped nest is built in the burrow. Made of dried grasses, this keeps the young well protected, snug and secure.

Before she gives birth, the female Wood Mouse drives off her mate. Then, after a 21-day gestation, she produces 2–9 blind, naked and helpless babies. At first she suckles them, and when they can walk she takes them out on feeding expeditions. Baby mice are prey to hundreds of hungry animals, birds and reptiles, so on these early forays the young bite hold of their mother's teats and run along abreast of her. At three weeks, however, the young are almost weaned, their eyes are wide open and they are becoming very active. By two months, those which have survived are themselves able to breed, and so the business of ensuring the survival of the species begins over again.

House Mice: Like the Wood Mouse, the common House Mouse is a very successful rodent. It originated in north Africa and southern Europe, but is now known all over the world. As its name suggests, the House Mouse seems happy to live around buildings, particularly food stores and granaries. House Mice will eat almost anything, and have even been found living happily in the sub-zero conditions of a meat freezer, eating the meat and nesting in the carcasses.

In one season, a female can give birth to around ten litters, of 5–7 young each, in a small round nest made of any soft, warm materials available. By the time the babies are 18 days old they are weaned, and at six weeks they become sexually mature themselves.

Harvest Mice: Unlike the House Mouse's comfortable ball of debris, the Harvest Mouse's home is an almost bird-like marvel of animal ingenuity. Suspended between strong stems, the nest is woven from leaves and blades of grass. It is spherical, almost completely enclosed, and has just enough room inside for the mother and her babies. At 16 days the young are weaned, and soon after they too begin to reproduce themselves.

Hamsters: Like rats and mice, hamsters are often kept as pets or used in laboratory experiments. However, most pet hamsters are the Golden variety, which has only ever been seen in the wild on two occasions in 1839 and 1930. The mother and 12 babies captured in Syria following the second sighting are, amazingly, the direct ancestors of *all* the Golden Hamsters now in captivity. Their staggering fertility—14–22 young per litter, after a gestation of only 15 days—is in contrast to the wild Common Hamster.

Found all over central Asia and Europe, these large (30 cm, 1 ft long), furry rodents live in shallow burrows made up of a central chamber with tunnels leading off to smaller living quarters. The female normally gives birth to only 7–8 helpless babies, and, of these, few survive a combination of 'natural' and human enemies. Those which do survive, though, are sexually mature

Left: The Hedgehog and the Grass Rat (below) are both born blind and deaf, but the former can move freely around by sense of smell whereas the latter is quite helpless.

and able to breed at three months.

Hedgehogs: Among the wealth of small mammalian life that lives in woods, gardens and hedgerows, one of the most singular creatures is the Old World Hedgehog. Like shrews and moles, Hedgehogs (also known as 'hedgepigs' and 'urchins') prefer a diet of insects, but they will eat a variety of food from berries to eggs or earthworms. Hedgehogs like to be warm, and when hibernating in colder weather or bringing up their young they retire to their nests of leaves and straw. These are found in a wide range of sites, from compost heaps to thick undergrowth, in fact wherever a comfortable hollow is to be found.

Baby Hedgehogs are born in the nest between May and July, after a gestation of 39–49 days. Each year one or maybe two litters of 3–7 young are born deaf, blind and sparsely covered with a few flexible white spines. For the first 24 hours the mother stays in the nest and suckles her young which—by their third day—are already beginning to grow a second coat of darker spines. Until they are around 11 days old,

Right: Baby Red Squirrels like this are born in litters of three or four in a special 'nursery' nest built by their mothers in a hole in a tree or among the branches. The new-born squirrels are blind and naked and for the first five or six weeks they need all the warmth the nest can give, together with their mother's life-giving milk.
Below: This young Grey Squirrel was also born blind and naked, but most probably in the drey or winter home of its mother, who does not bother to build a special nursery nest for her babies.
Below right: This fist-sized baby hare, in contrast, was born in the middle of a field with all its senses already acutely tuned, and wearing a warm coat of fur. At first it has to sit patiently in its nest, or 'form', all day until its mother arrives at night to suckle it, but within a few weeks even this contact is over and the little creature is on its own in a big, hostile world.

hedgepiglets are unable to roll into a defensive ball, because their muscles are not yet strong enough. If the mother has to leave the nest in search of food at this stage, she covers her babies with nest material; if she has to move them, she picks them up by the scruff of the neck and carries them.

At two weeks, the piglets' eyes open, and as the third and final set of spines grows, the remains of the first two drop out. By their fifth week the young can feed themselves, and the mother often leads them around in single file on foraging expeditions. A couple of weeks later they are weaned, and soon after they begin to wander off and start their own independent lives.

Hedgehogs are nocturnal, good swimmers and climbers, and hibernate from October–April. Despite their spiney defences, they are prey to predators like foxes, badgers, stoats, weasels and magpies which pull out their spines and peck away at the wounds. However, those babies which survive their foes, and the winter, are ready to reproduce when they are a year old.

Squirrels: Another small woodland mammal is the squirrel, of which there are over 70 species. They range from the mouse-sized Pygmy Squirrel of west Africa, to the American ground squirrels known as Chipmunks. Flying Squirrels—which do not actually fly, but glide—are nocturnal, unlike 'true' squirrels. Nonetheless, all squirrels are rodents, and they are most commonly seen in the early morning or just before dusk.

The Red Squirrel was once very common throughout Europe, but in recent years the more aggressive Grey Squirrel has taken over much of its territory. Nonetheless, those that remain usually build separate nests or 'dreys' for shelter and sleep as well as hibernation and rearing babies. The breeding-nest is made by the female, and is a covered structure of intertwined sticks, leaves and bark built into the branches of a tree or in a large hollow in a tree trunk.

There are two breeding seasons: the first from January–April and the second from early June–August. At these times, after a period of 30–40 days' gestation, litters of 3–4 (sometimes as many as 6) blind, naked young are born. After a week the babies' eyes open, and before long they are out with their parents in search of food. Those which survive nature's

hazards are able to breed after about a year.

Rabbits: Similar to rodents, but with an extra pair of incisor teeth, rabbits have many enemies, especially humans, but they have an amazing reproductive capacity. In fact, it has been calculated that one pair could have a possible 13 million descendants in just three years of successful breeding. Between January–June, a doe may have six litters of 2–10 babies each. The young arrive on a bed of straw or hay, warmly lined with fur stripped from the mother's underside, located in an underground burrow or on the surface in a shallow hole. Even though the babies are altricial at birth, the doe quickly camouflages her family and returns alone to the main burrow. Then, each night for three weeks, she returns to feed them, and by the time they are a month old the young are ready to begin lives of their own and the doe is probably once again pregnant.

Badgers: The Carnivora order of mammals includes such animals as weasels, stoats, dogs, cats, bears, otters and wolves—as well as badgers. Like most other Carnivorae, badgers are keen hunters, although they are also happy with a wide range of plant food. They live in a burrow (known as a 'set'), dug at least 3 m (10 ft) underground. It is made up of many rooms connected by long, winding passages and used for different purposes such as eating, sleeping or storing food. Badgers are scrupulously clean animals, and some time between February and May all the old straw and bracken bedding is replaced and the 1–5 cubs are born in a special 'nursery' chamber. When they are about eight days old the cubs' eyes open, but they do not venture out of the set until they are 6–8 weeks old. By this time their hair is darkening, and the characteristic black and white head stripes are becoming more pronounced. Mother badgers are protective of their

Left: This badger cub lives in one of nature's most opulent, multi-roomed burrows, especially compared with the Gerbils (above) who have only a bundle of grass for a home.

young long after they are weaned at around 12 weeks, and often family groups stay together until autumn, or even through the winter.

Shrews: More than 200 species of shrew are found around the world, and one of the most widespread varieties is the Common Shrew found in Europe and northern Asia. Between May and August, after a brief-encounter mating, the female weaves a cup-shaped nest of leaves, dry grass and other vegetation in a hole in the ground. Two to three weeks later she produces 4–10 young; however, as she only has six teats a maximum of six babies will survive. Those that do are weaned at 3–4 weeks and soon after they begin their own solitary lives, rooting through leaves and surface soil in search of insects, snails and worms.

Gerbils: This small nocturnal rodent (also known as the Sand Rat) is well adapted to life in the semi-desert areas of Africa and Asia, as most of its moisture requirements come from the seeds and grains on which it feeds. Like all other rodents, Gerbils are great hoarders and store large quantities of food in their burrows. When the babies are born they are blind and helpless. They grow quickly, however, and at six weeks are completely weaned and able to lead an independent existence.

41

Water babies

Otters: Among the land mammals that have returned to live in or near water are the 19 species of otter. These 'water-weasels' have webbed feet and streamlined bodies so they can hunt in rivers, streams, lakes and the sea. However, only one species is wholly marine.

The Common Otter of Europe and Asia breeds mainly in the spring, but cubs can be born at any time

Left: This young otter will be well equipped for a semi-aquatic life when it gets its waterproof under-fur after three months, whereas the non-specialized Raccoon family (below) simply likes to live near water, paddle and fish.

during the year. The breeding home—called a 'holt' or 'lair'—is only used as a nursery for the cubs, and at other times otters have no permanent homes. The holt is burrowed out of a bank with the entrance under water. The young are born there (5–9 of them), and they remain in the holt with their mother for two months while she suckles them.

Then, when the babies are old enough to enter the water, but are usually unwilling to do so, the mother has to coax them gently. If that does not work she will push them into the water, where they are soon playing

all day: sliding down the banks, chasing each other and diving for fish. Otters mainly eat fish, eels, frogs, newts and other aquatic creatures, but they can also hunt on land. This is especially useful when the water is iced over, and rabbits, birds, mice, voles and sometimes even farmyard chickens may be taken. In the absence of hunting or pollution, otters have few enemies and can expect to live for 10–12 years.

Sea Otters are found off the coasts of the North Pacific, spending much of their time near reefs and kelp beds, and only coming ashore during bad weather. Larger than other otters, Sea Otters have long luxuriant fur which is (unfortunately) highly prized by fashion-conscious people. Until protection laws came into force the number of Sea Otters was declining drastically.

When feeding, the Sea Otter floats on its back, using its chest as a table. Uniquely for otters, it also uses tools in the form of a stone which it carries up from the seabed and uses to crack open the shells of sea urchins or molluscs before eating them.

One baby is born at a time, and it is very soon introduced to the water and taught how to swim.

However, when her baby gets tired of swimming, the mother will turn on her back so that it can rest and suckle in her arms. Otherwise, the lives of baby otters on both land and water follow very similar courses.

Seals: The 32 species of seal are divided into two families: the eared seals and the earless, or true seals. The eared seals have small, externally visible ears taking the form of just a tiny flap, whereas the earless seals only have vestigial outer ears. Both types, however, have complete internal ear mechanisms. Seals are assumed to have evolved from land mammals, and they do have certain characteristics associated with them (ears, nose, fur, limbs, etc.) even though these have become modified for an aquatic life that may involve diving down almost 200 m (650 ft) and staying submerged for half an hour. Their diet includes squid, octopus and fish.

The 'earless' Atlantic, or Grey, Seal is mainly found along the coasts of the British Isles, particularly those of the Western Isles of Scotland and the Scilly Isles. The males arrive at the breeding ground to take up their territories well above the high-tide level at the beginning of September. A few weeks later the females

Above: The Antarctic Weddell Seal pup is born on the ice, but is truly one of the most aquatic of mammals.

(or 'cows' as they are known) arrive and give birth to their heavy babies weighing around 14 kg (30 lb) and covered with a thick white fur coat. The pups are suckled by their mothers, and gain about 2 kg (4½ lb) in weight per day from the rich fatty milk. After three weeks of this—during which time their mother has mated and begun yet another 9–12 month gestation period—the 50 kg (110 lb) pups lose their baby fur and take to the sea. Sometimes pups are born in a bull's territory, but he will take no notice of them and even shuffle his half-tonne mass right over them to get where he is going. The mothers, on the other hand, are attentive to their babies' every need, licking and suckling them and defending them from other jealous cows.

Harbour, or Common, Seal babies get much the same degree of care and attention, but they are born in water or in sand-spits or estuarine mud-banks at flood-tide level. They are well developed at birth, and within a few hours they are swimming away with their mother.

Hippopotamuses: Unlike the seal, the tropical African Hippopotamus is an amphibious mammal (the name is Ancient Greek for 'river-horse'). It spends much of its time during the day in shallow pools and rivers where colonies live and feed off aquatic plants and bask. The females, with their young, live in the centre of a lake or river, and each of the males has his own peripheral territory. Hippos can remain submerged for up to 10 minutes, swimming swiftly underwater or walking along the bottom. They come out on land mainly at night when their blue-grey skins act as effective camouflage, and individuals have been known to travel 48 km (30 miles) to find their chosen food.

Like other large mammals, Hippo mothers give birth (underwater) to a single baby weighing around 27 kg (60 lb) after a gestation period of 227–240 days. The baby is lovingly cared for and suckled underwater until it is about a year old. Its mother ensures its safety by carrying it on her back and then teaching it to swim at her shoulder. When she goes off to feed on land she leaves her baby in the care of one or two other females, who take charge of a crèche and baby-sit for all the mothers until they have finished feeding. A

45

Right: Among amphibian mammals, few have adapted to both terrestrial and aquatic lifestyles as well or as successfully as the Hippopotamus. From the moment of birth—which will almost certainly be in the water—young Hippos are equally at home in either environment. At first the mother keeps her baby at her shoulder as it ventures out to deep water, but it soon becomes accomplished both on and under the surface, often staying submerged for long periods to suckle its mother's milk. The baby rarely leaves its mother's side for the first years of its life, and this is perhaps as well because both land carnivores and crocodiles are always waiting to make a meal of a plump, young 'water-horse'.

major threat comes from the adult males, who are aggressive and will attack babies or each other at any opportunity. When it is old enough, the mother teaches her offspring to follow her on land, and the two will often stay together for five years before the baby has grown up and is able to fend for itself.

Water Voles: Although they are also known as 'water-rats', these little rodents are neither rats nor rat-like in any way. Semi-aquatic, and distinguished by their blunt, conical muzzles, and small ears, eyes and tails, they are also very short-sighted. Water Voles are found over most of Europe, where they burrow into the banks of streams and rivers. They feed on insects, snails and mussels as well as aquatic vegetation and, like most rodents, they store food in large quantities for times of scarcity. They usually stay close to their home burrow, and during the April–October breeding season a solid, globe-shaped nest of intertwined reeds and grasses is constructed by the female. The babies usually come in litters of five and are altricial at birth, although by the time they are three weeks old they are already independent. As they do not take naturally to the water they have to be taught to swim by their mother, who keeps them at her shoulder until they have become capable swimmers.

From then on it is not long before the babies themselves are breeding. However, as young Water Voles seem so reluctant to swim, it is hardly surprising that some choose to live entirely on land, only swimming between one land-based feeding area and another, or to escape from the many predators that beset them. In fact Water Voles are so vulnerable that they only have a life-expectancy of a year in the wild. Similar in habits and appearance to the Water Voles are the Water Shrews. However, these small aquatic rodents are not so well adapted, and as their fur is not waterproof they have to run through a tight little tunnel to their burrow to squeeze excess water from their coats.

Water fowls: Some birds are well adapted to a life spent near pools, swamps and marshes, where they generally build nests near or on the water. Of course there are exceptions, and although most water-birds are ground nesting, the Fairy Tern (found on Pacific islands) lays her one egg on a branch in a bush or a small tree where it is balanced as on a tightrope. When hatched, the tiny chick does not swim straight away, but remains on its branch for several days. Eventually it reaches the ground either by jumping or accidentally falling, and then takes to the water. Nonetheless, water fowl generally swim well, eat mainly aquatic grasses and insects, and may also dive.

One bird of this type is the European Water Rail found in Africa and northern Europe. Other species of rail are found in America, Australia and southern Africa, and the birds are about the size of a blackbird, with short tails and a long thin red beak. Rails build

Left: This very young Water Vole has bravely, or rashly, ventured into the open to sample the water. Having been born in a grass-lined nest at the end of a burrow in the bank, it is surprising that, like otters, young Water Voles are reluctant to get wet for the first time, and will often scream and protest until they can reach dry land again. However, the young—encouraged by their mother—soon overcome their fears and when they are three weeks old they are already independent, dividing their time between the land and the water and living off nuts and seeds, roots and waterside plants.

their bowl-shaped nests among the reeds where they are well hidden, and after three weeks of brooding—which the parents share—5–10 mauve-spotted, creamy-white eggs hatch. The babies are precocial and can leave the nest soon afterwards.

Moorhens are similar to rails in their choice of food and nest-sites, but they are less shy and are more often seen by humans. They are found almost everywhere except Australia. Baby Moorhens leave the nest two days after hatching and the little black chicks are soon swimming, watched closely by their parents.

Coots closely resemble Moorhens but are distinguishable by their dark plumage and white bills. They are not solitary, like rails, but are commonly seen in sociable communities with other birds on lakes and open water, often dipping underwater just long enough to grab their food. Coots normally have two or three clutches of 6–9 speckled, light-grey eggs in the breeding season which runs from May to August. They are laid either in a floating nest or in one fixed to weeds, and after an incubation period of 22–24 days the chicks hatch and soon after take to the water. There, they are often tended by their father alone if their mother is laying or brooding another clutch of eggs. In a further sociable gesture, the chicks from the first clutch will very often help their parents to rear their younger sisters and brothers.

Salmon: More than 23,000 species of fish are known

to exist, and collectively these cold-blooded creatures are considered to be the most ancient of vertebrates—those animals which have a spinal column. While most fish are perfectly adapted to aquatic life, either in fresh or salt water, most Salmon (along with Striped Bass, Sea and River Lampreys and Sturgeon) are anadromous: that is, they swim up-river from the sea to spawn. This transition is achieved with the help of adaptable gill and kidney mechanisms, and is also associated with changes in the brightness and tone of the fish's silvery-grey, red- and black-spotted skin. Atlantic Salmon, for example, swim up-river from the sea, fasting all the way, to the stretch of river in which they were born. At the breeding-ground the female makes a hole in the gravel and lays 700–800 eggs, which are simultaneously fertilized by sperm released from the male's body. Then she swims a little further upstream, 'cuts' another hole (using this gravel to cover the previous batch of newly-laid eggs), and lays another batch which the male fertilizes. The laying process goes on until the female has produced 700–800 eggs per half kilo (pound) of body weight at which point most of the males swim off, exhausted, and die. However, most females also never manage to return to the sea, although around 5 per cent are estimated to repeat the cycle and return years later to spawn again.

Meanwhile, after several weeks the eggs hatch and

the young stay feeding and growing in the river for 1–7 years; the time increases the more northerly the river. When the young are ready to go down to the sea a chemical component of their excrement (guanin) enters their skin, which changes to a bright silvery colour. Atlantic Salmon usually spend three or more years in the sea before seeking out their 'home' rivers and returning to spawn, overcoming all kinds of obstacles in their drive to reach the stretch of water in which they grew up.

In contrast, some species of Pacific Salmon leave the river soon after they hatch, head out to sea, and stay there until the time comes for their marvellous sense of smell to direct them back to spawn in the river which they left as tiny 'fry' years before. Other salmon varieties—the Atlantic Salmon in some parts of Scandinavia, and those in the Yugoslavian Dalmatian Alps, for example—live entirely freshwater lives.

Tadpoles: The three main groups of amphibians (Newts and Salamanders, Frogs and Toads and Caecilians) form an evolutionary link between fish and reptiles. Consequently, like fish, most amphibians lay eggs in water. However, the tadpoles which hatch at the larval stage and at first swim and breathe through gills like fish, quite soon develop lungs, arms and legs, and become air-breathing with the additional advantage that oxygen can be absorbed from water through their skin.

Of the amphibians, among the most widely distributed are the 2,600 varieties of frogs and toads. As a rule, female frogs simply lay their ready-fertilized eggs in a pond and leave them there to their fate; this means that they quite often provide food for a passing bird, fish or aquatic animal.

The Common Frog, for example, lays 1,000–2,000 eggs in a mass in a shallow pond in February or March. About four weeks later the surviving larvae hatch into tiny brown tadpoles which are so weak that they can hardly wriggle. At first they cling to water-weed using a special head sucker, while they finish what is left of their yolk-sac.

Soon after, in a remarkable metamorphosis, gill plumes develop, a mouth appears, lungs replace gill plumes, limbs grow and the tail is absorbed into the enlarging body. By 10 weeks the young frog is ready to take to the land, where it will feed on insects, slugs and worms.

Unlike the Common Frog, the female Common Toad lays her eggs in batches of three or four. Within a few days they have formed into gelatinous strings of 3,000–4,000 eggs, which hatch about 12 days later. After following much the same pattern of development as frog tadpoles, the surviving young toads leave the water after about 11 weeks. From then on, like frogs, they have to beware of such predators as weasels, rats, hedgehogs, birds and grass snakes.

Although the Common Frog and Common Toad follow the most usual pattern of reproduction and larval development, not all frogs and toads simply abandon their spawn. The Blacksmith Frog, for example, constructs a private watery nursery for its eggs; while the male Midwife Toad carries long strings of eggs in a tangle around his back legs until they hatch and swim off. The male of the Darwin Frog also behaves quite oddly: he swallows the eggs, which then develop into tadpoles in his swollen vocal sacs.

Like Frogs and Toads, Salamanders and Newts are found all over the world, but particularly in the northern hemisphere. Newts are smaller than salamanders, and spend more time in the water. However, both are similar to frogs and toads in their habits, although in their case the young do not re-absorb their tails into their bodies. During the breeding season the male newt emits the sperm, which then sinks. The female moves over it and it passes into her body where it fertilizes the eggs before they are laid. The eggs themselves are deposited on the leaves of water plants, and hatch after 21 days. Strangely, some newts reach maturity but remain permanently in the tadpole stage. One such well-known species is the Mexican Axolotl, which is the larval stage of the Tiger Salamander. Even in this completely aquatic tadpole stage—with branching gills and a rudder tail—the female Axolotls are still able to lay eggs which, in the proper conditions, will develop into young salamanders.

Finally, there are the Caecilians. These are worm-shaped, burrowing amphibians that tunnel under the earth and swim in streams in tropical countries. Unlike other amphibians they do not appear to conform to any set patterns: some young go through the aquatic larval stage, while others hatch in their adult form.

Turtles: Scientifically, there is no proper difference between Tortoises, Terrapins and Turtles. They all lay eggs resembling those of a bird, have poor hearing and keen sight, and are classed together as Chelonians —the most primitive group of reptiles. However, the popular names by which they are known vary wildly from country to country. The creature known as a Tortoise in Britain, for instance, is called a Turtle in America. The only workable solution appears to be to refer to all 250 species of Chelonians as Turtles, and to use specific names for specific species.

Marine turtles normally live in warm sea waters, but they come on land to lay their eggs which are left for the heat of the sun to incubate. For example, the female of the familiar Green Turtle, which is found in tropical and sub-tropical seas, drags herself up a sandy beach at night, digs a hole with her hind feet, and then lays up to 200 eggs over a period of about 14 days. Then she covers them with sand and leaves them to hatch— an operation made much easier for the babies by a little 'egg tooth' at the end of their snout which drops off soon after hatching. Many baby turtles are killed before they ever reach the sea by predators such as birds, rats and pigs. Adult Green Turtles, and their eggs, have also long been a favourite food of humans as well. As a result, Green Turtles are now unknown on many of the islands where they were once common.

In contrast, the European Pond Tortoise is a freshwater creature. Like other freshwater turtles it is only semi-aquatic, and spends most of its time around pond

Below: The Black Swan became so numerous in New Zealand earlier this century that large numbers were destroyed as pests.

and river banks feeding on fish, insect and amphibian food in the water—although it will also take rodents, small birds, worms, molluscs and crustaceans. Its limbs are web-footed and clawed, and it can be found in the Mediterranean areas of Europe, northern Africa and south-west Asia, where it grows up to 35 cm (14 in) in length. After an enforced summer mating in the water—which often amounts to sexual assault—the female usually lays 10 eggs in the soil, and then deserts them. After incubating for three or four months the eggs hatch, and the babies develop very slowly from then on. Many are lost to predators, and it may

be 15–20 years before females are mature, and 12–13 years for males.

The Snapper, commonly found in North America, is a large freshwater turtle (or terrapin) which grows to be about 50 cm (20 in) long. It spends most of its time submerged, only occasionally rising to the surface to breathe. Nonetheless, Snappers are very aggressive underwater, and as the name suggests they have strong, hooked jaws. Their diet is mainly of carrion, but also includes fresh fish, frogs and other amphibian flesh. Like other Chelonians, the Snapper's eggs are laid on land, where they hatch after 10 weeks.

Crocodiles: The ferocious crocodile, largest of reptiles, has the jaws and teeth to tear almost any animal to pieces. Despite this, however, females of the 16 species (including Caymans, Gharials, Alligators and true Crocodiles) are affectionate and considerate mothers. From the time they lay their eggs they keep a careful watch over their babies until they are several years old and living completely independent lives.

Crocodiles like hot weather, and different varieties are most common in the southern USA, Central and South America, southern Asia, northern Australia, India, Sri Lanka and the non-desert regions of Africa. One fairly typical example is the Nile Crocodile of Africa. This huge aquatic reptile may grow to be more than 5 m (16 ft) long, and is found on the banks of rivers, lakes, swamps and mud flats, where it lives in a lair at the end of a tunnel in a bank. It is basically nocturnal and hunts in the water at night. It can remain completely still on banks for hours, or lie motionless underwater with only the tip of its snout showing until an unsuspecting meal comes along for a drink. At this point the crocodile glides noiselessly to the water's edge, seizes its prey and knocks it senseless with its tail before dragging it into the water to be torn apart and eaten. Until baby crocodiles are about $1\frac{1}{2}$ m (5 ft) long and big enough to attack prey for themselves, their mothers normally bring pieces of meat to feed them. As crocodiles never stop growing, size is a good indicator of age, and some enormous 7-metre (23-ft) Nile Crocodiles have been estimated to be at least 50–60 years old.

The marine equivalent of the Nile Crocodile is the fearsome Estuarine variety. This lives on coasts stretching in an arc from Australia, through Indonesia, the Solomon Islands and the Philippines to India, Sri Lanka and Pakistan. Little is known of the life of babies of this species, except that when they grow up they often swim far out to sea. As their diet includes all meat—dead or alive—they can be a serious danger to humans in their 'home' waters. Estuarine Crocodiles are the world's largest living reptiles, and in the 19th century a 9-metre ($29\frac{1}{2}$-ft) monster weighing two tonnes was shot in the Philippines.

Left: This photograph shows a baby Nile Crocodile at the moment of hatching from its egg in a South African conservation breeding-station. To see such a tiny creature (the egg is less than 7½cm, 3in, long) struggling to break out of its shell, it is difficult to imagine that the very same reptile may one day become a ferocious 6½-m (20-ft) monster capable of killing or maiming any living creature that ventures within reach. However, even Nile Crocodiles have enemies at this early stage of their lives and most of the 60 or so babies that would, in the wild, have hatched from the same clutch as this one would have been killed by predatory birds and mammals.

Left: This pair of young Flat-backed Turtles are members of one of the rarest species of the world's marine Chelonians. Very few of these turtles have ever been sighted in the warm waters of northern Australia where they live. This is probably because only about one in every 1,000 of the babies that hatch from the leathery-shelled eggs laid in the sand will live to lay its own eggs on that same beach some four years in the future.

Far left: Baby turtles improve their chances of survival when they dig themselves out of the sand at night.

Tree-living babies

Woodland and forest obviously offer abundant food and shelter to a wide range of animals, and many mammals have consequently adapted to a specialized, tree-dwelling (or arboreal) existence. Some of them rarely, if ever, descend to the ground, whereas others spend only a proportion of their time climbing and hunting for food among trees and bushes.

Opossums: While some species of opossum are arboreal, others are terrestrial, and the Water Opossum is an aquatic variety. Most opossums, however, are marsupials; that is, their babies are born at an early stage of development and crawl up their mother's fur until they reach a special pouch inside which the mother's teats are located. The babies enter this pouch and each takes into its mouth a teat, which then expands and anchors it firmly. The young stay inside the pouch for some two months or more by which time they have developed sufficiently to face the outside world. However, not all opossums have pouches. For example, the Murine species found from Mexico to Brazil suckles its young in a conventional mammalian manner.

The Virginian or Common Opossum is a nocturnal marsupial about 45 cm (17 in) long which sleeps in tree-holes or burrows in the day, has a rat-like appearance and a prehensile tail. It is a very successful creature, and in the last few thousand years it has extended its range from South to North America. It lives on a diet of insects, smaller mammals, eggs and birds, fruit, carrion and grain, and is considered a pest because of the damage it does to crops.

Two litters are born each year, the first in February and the second in June. Up to 20 babies are born each time, after a gestation of 13 days. At birth the peanut-sized young crawl into their mother's pouch, and the lucky ones each gain possession of one of the 13 teats. Those not so lucky soon die, and in the end 7–8 babies emerge after 60–70 days of rapid growth in the pouch.

From there they crawl up on to their mother's back and cling on tightly as she moves around until they are big enough to go off on their own.

Flying Lemurs: In spite of superficial resemblances to bats and the lemur family of primates, the Flying Lemur is in no way related to either group. Found

Left: A young, arboreal Virginian Opossum, North America's only living marsupial which has extended its range from South America.
Right: A young Slow Loris is left clinging to a branch in a Malayan forest while mother goes off to feed.

in the wooded parts of south-east Asia, southern China and the Philippines, this creature has become so used to living high in the trees that its specialized limbs are now useless for walking on the ground; instead it creeps along in much the same way as a bat. It has an arresting appearance with large eyes and ears, a slender body about 65 cm (26 in) long covered with greyish-brown fur, and a gliding membrane which consists of skin attached to its shoulders, arms, ankles and tail.

Despite its name, the Flying Lemur does not fly, but leaps then glides from tree to tree. In this way it can travel up to 90 m (100 yd) in a single 'flight'. During the day it sleeps, hanging upside down flat against a tree. The babies are born singly after a gestation of two months, and from their first day they have to hang on tightly with their five strong digits to their mother's underside fur as she leaps from tree to tree. Occasionally a baby will be left alone on a branch while its mother is feeding, however as dawn breaks and dangers multiply it is time for the family to go to sleep, and throughout the day the adult hangs from a branch, making a comfortable hammock for the baby out of its body.

Slow Lorises: These slow-moving, deliberate climbers are seldom seen by human eyes. They belong to the primate Sub-order of Prosimians (meaning 'pure' or 'early' monkeys), and the name 'Loris' is derived from the Dutch *loeris*, meaning 'clown'. Solitary, lemur-like Slow Lorises are found in the dense forests of India, Sri Lanka and south-east Asia, where they rarely leave the tree-tops. They are nocturnal, and

in the daytime they roll into a ball and cling to a branch, sleeping with their head tucked into their knees. They have large eyes which admit plenty of light, and a naked, moist nose similar to that of a dog. The close, thick, woolly fur varies in colour from brownish-red to silver-grey depending on the environment. The animal's diet includes insects, small animals and fruit.

When a baby is born (and there is usually only one), it is carried along clinging to its mother's underside, and sometimes when she is feeding it will be left on a branch to wait until she finishes. As it gets older the baby is promoted to riding on its mother's back, and this practice continues until it is almost the size of its parents.

Bushbabies: These African prosimians are closely related to lorises. The six species are also known as galagos or 'Night-apes', and vary from the size of a mouse to that of a domestic cat. They have long hind limbs that can propel them over 2 m ($6\frac{1}{2}$ ft) high from a standing start, and long tails for balance which enable them to hop around like kangaroos on the ground. They are nocturnal, and sometimes sleep in communal nests in the fork of a tree.

Usually a solitary baby is born in a nest after a gestation of 130–135 days, but sometimes there are

Left: A full-grown bushbaby would easily sit in the palm of a person's hand, so the tiny size of these prosimian babies can easily be imagined. Below: This young White-faced Tamarin is related to the Marmosets, which used to be favourite pets of the 18th century nobility.

as many as three babies. When they are strong enough they leave the nest and cling tightly to the fur on the mother's underside as she moves around the branches, from time to time leaping across from one tree to another. Bushbaby young, like young lorises, are sometimes left alone while their mothers go off to feed.

Vervet Monkeys: Because of its wide distribution throughout south-east African forests, this monkey is known by several alternative names, principally as the Green Monkey or Grivet depending on the locality. It is a true arboreal, seldom descending to the forest floor but travelling through the trees in bands or family groups led by an old male. Each band has its own territory which is jealously guarded, and any intruding bands or individuals are speedily driven away. Vervet Monkeys eat fruits, wild honey, shoots, leaves and the occasional bird's egg or nestling, although farmers regard them as pests because of their penchant for raiding cultivated fields.

These primates breed continuously, and after a six-month gestation one or two babies are born. The young are lovingly cared for by their mothers, who regularly cuddle them and comfort them as they cling on to her fur when the band is on the move. As it gets older the baby has to be taught to climb, and by its sixth month it will almost be weaned. From then on the young monkey gradually passes through stages of childhood and adolescence, eventually establishing an adult role in its extended family grouping.

Orang-Utans: These apes, smaller only than Gorillas, live peaceful lives in the densely-forested upland and lowland regions of Sumatra and Borneo. Sadly, however, their numbers are diminishing all the time as humans continue to trap the young for export—often killing the breeding mothers in the process. As a result, Orang-utans are now in imminent danger of extinction from the wild, and it is estimated that less than 5000 of them remain.

They are wonderfully adapted to an arboreal life and progress through the trees using all four limbs; they have long curved fingers which hook over branches with ease while they hang and swing from their arms and legs. In fact, their feet are not really used as feet at all, but more as a second pair of hands.

Orang-utans live singly, in pairs or in small family groups. They are diurnal and before they settle down at night they build a platform in a tree on which to sleep. This temporary shelter is made up of small branches, roughly interlaced and trampled well down in a tree-fork. Male Orangs (at $1\frac{1}{2}$ m, 5 ft) are twice as tall as females, and weigh around 70 kg (150 lb). The males often travel through the trees alone, but females are always accompanied by one or two of their babies —one already half grown from a previous breeding season.

At birth the babies weigh less than 1 kg (2 lb), and they are nursed by their mothers until they are 18 months old. They receive constant care and attention but, when they are two years old, they nonetheless go off on their own. By the time they are eight years old young Orangs are sexually mature, but they will not

Left: The female Orang-utan is one of the most loving and devoted of all mothers. She normally stays with her single child from the time it is born until it is weaned at four years of age. During this period, she teaches it everything it needs to know about how to live in the forest, even occasionally making trips down to the ground with it to practise walking. Here though, in a rare moment, a baby Orang has been photographed alone engrossed in the business of learning how to chew and feed on a leaf-bearing stalk broken from a nearby tree. Right: A young Grey Squirrel shows just how easy it is to run down a tree-trunk if you have the right sort of claws on your feet. This species originated in North America, but has now spread to Europe where it is considered a major woodland pest. It has done much to reduce dramatically the number of Red Squirrels by succeeding in competition for the same teritories.

be fully grown until they reach 12 years of age.

Grey Squirrels: Of the two best known varieties of squirrel (the Red and the Grey), the Grey Squirrel is the larger, with untufted ears and a less bushy tail. Originally a native of North America, this variety was introduced to the British Isles as a pet in the 19th century. Being an aggressive species, Grey Squirrels have since gone back to the wild in Britain and multiplied rapidly.

Grey Squirrels are diurnal, good swimmers, can climb well and also run like a flash down tree trunks or jump from tree to tree. They feed on buds, berries, nuts, mushrooms, acorns, bird's eggs and nestlings. Like other rodents they collect food in preparation for those warmer winter days when they will arouse from their slumbers (they do not hibernate, strictly speaking) and feel like a meal. The items of their stores are buried singly in the ground and can be located much later—even under thick snow—by sense of smell.

During the breeding season which lasts from late December to August, two litters of 3–7 babies are born, blind and naked in a specially constructed nursery nest. Their eyes open after about a month, and 2–4 weeks later they are weaned. At 10 weeks they are independent, but the young do not reach sexual maturity until they are about eight months old. In the wild, Grey Squirrels live for around eight years unless they succumb to predators.

Dormice: The several species of Dormouse are Old World creatures preferring an arboreal environment, and their babies develop along similar lines.

The Common Dormouse is about the size of a mouse, and it lives in deciduous woodlands in Scandinavia, Europe and Asia Minor. It is nocturnal and climbs actively at night, spending its days asleep in specially constructed sleeping-nests made of dry leaves, moss and bark. These spherical-shaped nests (there are maybe 5–6 per season) are usually constructed in bushes, tree hollows, or beneath a tussock of grass. In contrast, the dormouse's breeding-nest is twice the size of its sleeping-nests, and it is used exclusively by the mother and her young, as she drives off her mate to a sleeping-nest of his own as soon as she becomes pregnant. After 25 days gestation, 3–4 babies are born, naked and blind. When they are 18 days old their eyes open and they are weaned at one month. After 40 days the young are independent, and by the time they are a year old they themselves can breed. Dormice usually have several litters in the spring and summer season. However, as they hibernate from late October to April, autumn litters usually do not have time to build up the fatty reserves they need to survive for such a long period without food. In any case, dormice fare poorly through hibernation and only one out of five wake up in spring, the rest having become food for foraging non-hibernators.

58

Tropical babies

Some of the world's most unusual and interesting creatures are to be found in the zone between the Tropics of Cancer and Capricorn. Animal life there is an endless round of searching for food, water, shade and refuge from relentless insect and animal predators. Many of these animals are physically strong, generally they have keen senses, and most are born at an advanced state of development. They also have to be quick witted, cunning and well organized to survive in a mostly hostile, ever-shrinking world.

Rhinoceroses: There are five surviving species of rhinoceros, all closely related to the horses, asses, tapirs and zebras. The Black and White varieties are found in central and southern parts of Africa; the Sumatran, Indian and Javan species are found in the Orient. These animals have marvellous senses of hearing and smell, but they have poor vision. Nonetheless, they share one unique feature: they have horns on their faces which grow from the skin on the mid-line of their bodies. These horns are formed by a rounded mass of hairs solidly attached to a rough outgrowth of bone. Both the African and the Sumatran varieties have two horns (one may be much larger than the other), while the Indian and Javan Rhinos have only one.

In spite of their tough skin, rhinos are extremely sensitive to insect bites. To circumvent this problem they take regular mud baths, and are then protected to some extent by the thick crust of mud which insects have difficulty in penetrating.

While most rhinos are solitary and peaceful, content to browse among the twigs, leaves, scrub and young shoots, the massive Black Rhino is aggressive and often attacks without provocation. It differs from the White Rhino in that its upper lip is elongated and prehensile and is used in much the same way as an elephant's trunk.

Above left: A young rhino has an ungainly romp with its massive mother, who takes sole parental responsibility for her baby's upbringing.
Left: Even a young gnu as small as this will be living almost independently, only communicating with mother through her udder.

This creature measures $3-3\frac{3}{4}$ m (10–12 ft) from the tip of its nose to the root of its tail, and it weighs up to a staggering 1·8 tonnes. Its skin colour varies from pale grey to dark brown, and its front horn—generally a good deal longer than the rear one—can measure as much as 60 cm (2 ft).

The Black Rhino ranges across Angola, Rhodesia, Kenya, Tanzania and Uganda, but each individual stays fairly close to its home base in the area of thorny scrub where it finds most of its food. It is partially nocturnal and likes to sleep under a shady tree or in a thicket. Tickbirds remain in attendance on it as it sleeps, doing the rhino a useful service by searching through its thick skin and eating the troublesome parasites, while also getting a good meal for themselves at the same time.

After mating, the female Black Rhino has to wait about 17 months until her baby is born, and consequently she can only have one every other year. At birth the baby is relatively tiny (only 50 cm, 20 in, high) but—like most babies with hooves—it is able to stand up within its first few hours and suckle milk from its mother. A few days later it is able to follow its mother to her favourite water-hole and, at the end of a week, it can browse for its food even though it is not yet weaned.

The other species of tropical African rhino is the White variety. Needless to say, like the Black Rhino which is not really black, the White Rhino is not really white, but a shade of grey. However, it is the only rhino species which grazes, and although it is larger than all the others it is not in the least bit aggressive and is, in fact, quite friendly. Its breeding behaviour is similar to that of the Black Rhino; once again the mother takes all the parental responsibilities.

Buffaloes: Like all ruminants, buffaloes chew the cud, have four-chambered stomachs and an efficient digestive tract. African Buffaloes represent one of the largest families of that continent's animals, and they are distributed widely south of the Sahara. Like rhinos, buffaloes like to take mud baths, and for the same reason too. The appearance of buffaloes varies greatly depending on their environments, which range

from dense tropical jungles to the semi-arid savannah. In the past, naturalists have been mistaken in believing the difference in appearance to be indicative of separate species. However, it is now known that they are not really separate species at all, but varieties of the same one.

Whatever the environment, an African Buffalo is a very dangerous creature to tangle with, as many hunters and lions have found to their cost. In fact many have not lived to tell the tale, as buffaloes are very easily provoked into goring an enemy with their horns or alternatively kicking and trampling them to death.

The Cape, or Black, Buffalo—with its huge spreading horns—is the largest variety, weighing in at just under a tonne, and standing 2 m (6½ ft) tall to the shoulder. It grows to a maximum of 3 m (10 ft) measured from the tip of its nose to the root of its tail. After a gestation period of around 11 months, the mother gives birth to one or two babies which arrive with their eyes open and the ability to stand. Within a few hours of being born they are able to run with the herd, and for several months calves remain close to their fiercely protective mothers.

Brindled Gnus (or Blue Wildebeests): These animals, commonly known as Wildebeests, live on open grassy plains ranging across South Africa, the Transvaal, Mozambique and Rhodesia. Although they are a species of antelope, Wildebeest look more like a cross between a bull and a pony, featuring large pointed horns which curve round and over their heads. Those horns belonging to the males (longer than the females') sometimes measure as much as 1 m (3 ft) along the curve. During the dry season various small herds band together to form a large herd of 100–150 individuals, often mixed in with zebras and other antelopes. This large group often migrates long distances from one water-hole to the next, or from an exhausted grazing area to a new, richer one. On the open plains, though, the gregarious Wildebeests have a formidable foe in the mighty lionesses and lions. Nonetheless, the Wildebeest's keen sight and excellent sense of smell means that predators have to work hard to catch their meal unawares.

The baby Wildebeests are born 8–9 months after conception. Like most other babies born surrounded by predators, they are well developed, able to see, and able to stand up practically straight away. So, if the calf is healthy and strong it has a good chance of surviving because it may have to run with the herd half an hour after its birth. However, if it is sick or weak and unable to run it may be left behind with its mother, who will not usually desert her offspring even in the face of danger. If this happens, both mother and calf would be lucky to last long before falling prey to lions, wild dogs, hyenas or other hunting predators.

Left: This newly-hatched Ostrich is 30cm (1ft) tall; in another 18 months it will be a 2m (7ft) tall adult.
Above: An African Elephant mother makes for the bush with her young baby, urging it on with the aid of her trunk.

Elephants: The largest land mammals on this planet are the elephants. The female Indian Elephant is the smallest member of the species yet she is still larger and heavier than any other male land mammal. Despite their size, these massive creatures run very quickly over short distances, and also feel quite at home in water. They are vegetarian, feeding on branches, leaves, fruits and shoots for up to 18 hours every day. The food is conveyed to their mouths by their highly sensitive, prehensile, elongated noses—their trunks.

Each African Elephant has two triangular shaped 'lips' or 'fingers' on the end of its trunk, with which to grip small delicate objects; while Indian Elephants have only one 'lip' or 'finger'.

Elephants find hundreds of uses for their trunks, including smelling, touching, feeding, drinking, spraying themselves with dust in dust-baths, and taking showers. Also, their skin is very thick, but is nonetheless sensitive to both insect-bites and the heat of the sun, which dries it out and causes it to chap. So elephants, like rhinos and buffaloes, frequently bathe and roll in mud.

African Elephants are larger than Indian Elephants, and the average height of the male (measured to his shoulders) is just over $3\frac{1}{4}$ m ($10\frac{1}{2}$ ft), compared with an average male Indian Elephant at 3 m ($9\frac{3}{4}$ ft). In both cases the females are slightly smaller, averaging 3 m ($9\frac{3}{4}$ ft) in the African variety and 2·15 m (7 ft) for the Indian cow.

There are several other distinguishing features between African and Indian Elephants, and probably the most obvious is the much larger size of the African Elephant's ears. This species also has a steeply sloping head and much larger tusks. These tusks are actually upper incisor teeth which extend down on either side of the trunk, although in female Indian Elephants they are almost non existent. In addition, the Indian Elephant has a high domed forehead which is the highest point on its body, whereas the African species' shoulders are their highest body point.

Both species live in herds, the African Elephant in the savannahs of tropical Africa and the Indian Elephant in the forests and grasslands of southern Asia and Sumatra. During the rainy season in Africa and the monsoon in southern Asia, elephants often migrate long distances to find new feeding grounds. With their huge appetites they very soon exhaust food sources and are constantly on the move in search of fresh pastures. The herds travel in single file at a fairly slow pace, each animal swaying from side to side as first the two right feet move forward together and then the two left ones.

Elephants develop at much the same rate as humans: a cow is able to breed by the time she is 12 and a bull by the time he is 15. However, the gestation period for elephants, at 20–23 months, is extremely long by human standards. When the mother elephant feels that her baby is about to be born, she retires to a secluded bush or thicket with two other females from the herd, whose role apears to be that of protection against predators who would find the calving mother and her new-born baby relatively easy prey.

After a while the mother gives birth to a loose-skinned, pinkish-coloured, hairy baby which is 1 m (3 ft) tall and weighs about 90 kg (200 lb). The calf is dropped onto soft damp soil or a bed of leaves, and there it stays for a few hours, resting after its journey into the world. Within a few hours, though, the baby elephant is able to stand, and at two days it can walk. It is suckled by its mother long after it is able to feed itself, and final weaning does not take place until it is two years old. Because of their extremely long gestation period, female elephants are only able to have a baby every other year.

Baboons: Many species of these intelligent, savage and powerful monkeys are found throughout the African continent, and Arabia also has the Sacred Baboons which live on both sides of the Arabian Gulf. All baboons are large and have enormous strength, and with their long canine fangs the males (especially the old ones) can inflict serious injuries or often kill those whom they choose to attack.

Baboons are terrestrial animals that move about on all-fours and live in large, male-dominated communities in rough, open, rocky regions. The old males are the dominant force within the community, and they organize and discipline their large, complex, family troops. The attitudes held by the males toward the females are brutal and patriarchal; the male is so jealous of his mate that he will kill her if she is unfaithful to him.

The baboons' natural enemies are lions, leopards and human beings; however, they themselves can be just as dangerous as leopards. For example, the Chacma Baboon—which is the largest of them all and is found in South Africa—has a habit of killing and disembowelling young lambs and kids to drink the milk inside their stomachs. Normally though, baboons eat fruit, leaves, young shoots, insects and small reptiles. They also have cheek pouches where they are able to store food temporarily.

The Yellow Baboon species lives in east and central Africa in large, multi-male communities. It can be distinguished easily from others by its yellowish buff-coloured fur and long legs. Yellow Baboons are farm-raiders in some districts, helping themselves to growing crops and often threatening the farmworkers.

Their young are born after a gestation period of 154–183 days and at first the baby clings to its mother's underside, constantly holding one teat in its mouth and suckling from time to time. Later, when it is older, the baby rides on its mother's back from place to place, and although it may look friendly and docile at this stage, it will without doubt become surly and aggressive when it gets older.

Giraffes: This animal, the tallest living mammal, is found over all sub-Saharan Africa. Its neck is long, not because of extra vertebrae, but because of an increase in the length of each one. It has a long, black, prehensile tongue which extends to 50 cm (20 in) and is used in conjunction with the lips (which are also prehensile) to pluck leaves and branches off trees. The Giraffe's large, liquid brown eyes are set at the side of its head and, shaded and protected by long lashes, they provide a good field of vision which combines with its excellent hearing to give it an advantage over its smaller predators. It has between two and four horns on its forehead. These horns are covered with

Above right: On the open African savannah a mother Giraffe keeps an eye on the photographer as her offspring trustingly follows on behind.
Right: A group of Yellow Baboons, native to the tropical regions of central and southern Africa, gather around a pink-faced infant who has not yet developed the species' characteristic dog-like features, but who will for many months yet be carried about clinging to its mother's fur.

skin except for the tips which are hard, black and calloused.

Male Giraffes can grow to a height of $5\frac{1}{2}$ m (18 ft), while females are about $\frac{1}{2}$ m (20 in) shorter. Some Giraffes live in polygamous herds containing up to 20 individuals and consisting of a male, his harem and the babies. Others live in larger herds but these still contain a majority of females. Because of the long gestation period (14–15 months) female Giraffes breed once every two years.

At birth, the baby is 2 m ($6\frac{1}{2}$ ft) tall. The mother is standing during the delivery so the baby drops quite a distance before hitting the ground. Nonetheless it manages to rise to its feet after about an hour and then soon starts to suckle. Before it is a day old the baby Giraffe is able to run, and after just a few weeks it begins to feed itself with leaves and twigs while continuing to suckle until it is about six weeks old. Meanwhile a few weeks after its birth, the baby goes

to play with other baby Giraffes in a crèche which is closely supervised by two adults. However, it returns to its mother for milk, and later—when it is weaned—for companionship. When it is about a year old it finally leaves her and sets out on the three-year road to adulthood in its tall, communal society.

Down on the farm

Nowadays, almost all forms of human social organization involve agriculture, and the remaining groups of people who rely purely on hunting and gathering become fewer all the time. In some areas of the world the agricultural emphasis is on producing food or cash crops (like rice or hemp) directly from the land; in other areas livestock are reared, both for human nourishment and a wide range of non-edible resources. Much agriculture, however, involves a combination of livestock and crop cultivation. Nonetheless, in the Western world particularly, a relatively new phenomenon is the 'factory farm'. Such establishments make little reference to the natural behaviour of the animals they keep, only to the maximization of production and profit. Calves, piglets or chickens, especially, are born, reared, tended and then killed in closed conditions, without ever even seeing natural daylight. The suffering that goes with factory farming is justified by human values based on a taste for meat (or eggs, in the case of hens).

Calves: Factory farming aside, life down on most farms revolves around a close association with mature, young and baby animals. Probably the most useful of all animals to people have been the domesticated cattle. Throughout the world, calves are reared for one or more of three purposes: as milk producers, meat producers or—in the case of oxen and Indian Buffaloes, for instance—as beasts of burden or draught animals. Specialized breeds of cattle abound, with some, like the Channel Island breed, being particularly good milkers and others, like Herefords, being particularly good at putting on muscle rapidly for beef.

Traditionally, a farmer has a herd of cows producing milk, and a carefully-chosen bull that is used to 'serve'

Left: This beautifully-coloured young Jersey heifer calf is a valuable commodity to a dairy farmer, as the milk she will be producing within the next three years is among the richest in cream of any dairy breed. Until then, the calf will have an easy life along with others of its own age who only have to worry about enjoying themselves and eating plenty of good, rich food. Often, when a young cow has had her first calf, and then encounters a milking-machine for the first time, she becomes very uneasy and frisky. However, she soon gets used to the experience and before long she will join the rest of the dairy herd in walking unprompted into her own milking stall every morning and evening. Had the calf been a young bull, his prospects would not have been so rosy, as only a tiny minority are retained for breeding.
Right: A pair of day-old chicks who look so attractive at that age, but will probably be dirty, emaciated husks by the time they leave the battery house 18 months after their arrival.

all the herd. Young bulls are sexually mature at two, and cows at about the same age. Until they have had a calf, young cows are known as 'heifers', and having calved—after a nine-month gestation—they immediately start to give milk from their large four-teated udders. Cows give birth in a standing position, and the little calf emerges with its head between its front legs after what can often be a long and difficult labour. Many farmers leave their cows to calve in an open field if the weather is not too harsh, and in this case just before giving birth the cow usually walks away from the rest of the herd to a quiet part of the field.

Nowadays, bulls' semen can be stored under refrigeration, and many smaller farms no longer keep their own bulls, as they obviously cost a lot to feed and can often be difficult to manage; an angry or bad-tempered bull is a very dangerous animal indeed! Instead, centres exist where good-pedigree bulls are kept, and when a farmer wants a cow to be 'put in calf' a telephone call brings a veterinary officer from one of these centres, equipped with bull's semen and special equipment with which to artificially inseminate the cow.

One result of this practice has been a general improvement in the quality of calves, although there are also occasional side effects. A Friesian cow that has been crossed with a Charollais bull, for example, will produce a big calf that, if male, will rapidly gain weight for beef production, or be an adequate milker if female. However, such a big calf is often too large for its mother to deliver herself, and many times the farmer has to attach a rope to the calf's front feet and firmly pull it out in rhythm with its mother's labour contractions.

Normally, calves weigh around 14 kg (30 lb) at birth, and at first they are weak and covered in placental fluid and membrane. However, the mother at once starts to lick her baby clean and dry, and usually within an hour—as befits its plains-living ancestry—the little calf is able to struggle to its feet and suckle the very thick, rich, yellow milk that fills its mother's udder for the first day after giving birth. Calves can see from the start, and within a few hours they are strong enough

to trot around and keep up with their mother.

It is very unusual for twin calves to be born, and in such cases one (or both) of them is often very small and weak and will not normally survive without a great deal of special attention. Where cattle are kept in a semi-wild state, for beef production on ranches or the South American Pampas, for example, calves suckle their mother's milk for about six months before this supply dries up, although they will also have been grazing as well from their first weeks of life. However, in most countries milk itself is one of the most valuable cattle products, and in such cases calves will normally be separated from their mothers after their first day or two, by which time the cow's milk has stabilized into roughly equal proportions of cream, protein and sugar, and has become acceptable for human consumption.

This separation is sudden and final, and often leaves both the calf and its mother deeply distressed and protesting loud and long. Nonetheless calves grow quickly into either heifers or young bulls, nourished on enriched milk-substitutes, grass and

chemical additives. Male calves especially are often killed after only a few weeks for prime, pale veal, before they have had a chance to eat grass and darken the colour of their meat. The alternative is for them to be reared for at least another 18 months for beef, however this is expensive and if the farmer does not feel sure of good future beef prices then early slaughter is normally the financially sensible thing to do. Otherwise, male calves that are wanted for beef—not breeding—are castrated and fattened up for later slaughter. Castrating the males produces bullocks, which tend to put on weight more quickly than young bulls, and are also less prone to bad temper or aggression.

Small calves are appealing creatures, which love to suck milky fingers or play together, running around and butting their peers. In good weather they can happily be left to live and graze in fields, but when it is cold and wet, or in winter, they are kept indoors and fed on hay, silage and other compound foods rich in minerals and vitamins. They grow quickly, and at a year a calf from an average-sized breed will already

Left: A New Forest Pony foal lies on the ground where it was born only a few hours before. Having eaten the placenta, the foal's mother is now continuing to lick her baby clean and dry of all the birth fluid and membranes. This practice also serves to stimulate the new-born's nervous system in much the same way as a human baby is stimulated to cry at birth. Many of these ponies roam free in parts of southern England, and many more are also sold to be used for riding or as light draught animals for pulling small carts belonging to street traders. Right: A good-looking dappled mare and her handsome foal which shows signs of having Arab blood in its veins. The breeding and rearing of such horses is a big business in many countries where there is a high demand for hunters, racehorses and show-jumpers.

stand about 1 m (3–4 ft) at the shoulders. A year later, depending on the breed, the conditions and the food supply, the calves will be young adults standing almost as high as their parents.

At this stage male calves are intensively fattened ready for slaughter, and heifers are normally put into calf for the first time. After her first calf, a cow produces less milk during her first lactation than she will later when she is older. Using intensive feeding and farming methods, a prime cow of a good dairy breed like the Friesian will produce over 4500l. (1000 gallons) a year, with one six-month lactation followed by a short rest, another calf, and another lactation.

Although most domesticated cattle would live naturally for well over 20 years, down on the farm those that have survived are usually becoming either inefficient milkers or tired, aggressive bulls by their mid-to-late teens and are slaughtered.

Chicks: Wherever they are found, most farms around the world will have their share of poultry. Fowl are very popular because they can acclimatize to conditions ranging from the poles to the equator, and their numbers vary from just a few running around the farmyard, to several hundred living 'free range' in a field, to perhaps many thousands caged in batteries. In addition, ducks, geese and turkeys are often kept as farm poultry.

Farmyard fowl come in many breeds and varieties, varying greatly in colour and appearance. All of them, however, are kept either for meat or eggs or, most commonly, for both. Under natural conditions where hens and cocks live together, they mate during the breeding season and 4–10 chicks are born after a three-week incubation in a rough nest of straw and grass on the ground or on a low ledge. Within a few hours of emerging from the egg, the chicks dry off and turn into pretty, chirping balls of fluff. They soon

Left and above: Lambs like these are reared in enormous numbers on farms around the world (and on sheep stations in Australia and New Zealand) primarily for their meat but also for the value of their wool and skins.

leave the sanctuary of their mother's body and begin running around and pecking away merrily. It seems that the noisy chirps produced by chicks are very important recognition signals, as a mother hen who is cut off from the sound—but not the sight—of her chicks will make no effort to tend to them. Conversely, the young chicks are imprinted in their first hours of life with the image of their mother, who they will then follow around wherever she goes. However, if the chicks happen to see some other moving object before their mother (like a person or another farmyard bird), they are imprinted with the idea that that is their mother, and will behave accordingly. Either way though, cocks, who may mate with 15–30 hens, play no part in the upbringing of their chicks.

By the time they are 6–8 months old, the chicks themselves are virtually adult. At this point the surplus males are normally taken out of the farmyard to avoid endless fighting with the dominant cocks, and the young hens will begin to lay. In normal conditions, if fresh free-range eggs are collected each day, the hens will repeat the process and lay again after only a few days thereby ensuring a constant supply of eggs for the farmer.

Many modern farms do not keep free-range hens, but instead confine their egg-producing birds in batteries. Each cage in a battery may have 1–4 birds crammed in, and as the floors are sloping the eggs roll away to be collected as soon as they are laid. However as hens have an instinct to brood on eggs, they can be induced to lay as many as 5–6 per week under ideal battery conditions of controlled food, heat and light.

Chicks for batteries usually arrive at the farm in cardboard boxes containing several dozen when they are one day old. They have come from factories where thousands of hens are mated and their eggs scientifically incubated until they hatch. A highly-skilled human 'sexer' then sorts out the female chicks from the new-born cocks. The females that go to farms in spring to be reared for the batteries are ready to lay by autumn. With rich, expensive grain-based food they can then produce up to 5–6 eggs per week for a year, by which time they are exhausted, passed their best, and ready to be killed and turned into soup or roasting fowl. The male chicks from the hatchery, meanwhile, are either killed straight away or castrated (made into capons) and fattened for the table.

Many farmers also keep some turkeys, geese or ducks, all for the table, and the geese and ducks also for their large richly-yolked eggs and sometimes even the value of their feathers and down. Young turkeys, goslings and ducklings hatch from their eggs after four weeks of incubation, and at birth they are open to the same imprinting phenomenon as domesticated fowl. Fed well and kept free of disease, the babies fatten quickly for the table. After 3–5 months they have normally reached a sufficient weight to be killed, although the adults are at their best for breeding purposes between 3–8 years of age.

Lambs: Springtime down on the farm is lambing-time, when the farmer has to go out every night in all weathers to check that the ewes are not in difficulties giving birth. Different individuals and breeds of sheep tend to have more or less lambs, and although twins are common and triplets or even quads not unknown, a farmer who averages two healthy lambs per ewe per year is doing very well. Lambs usually weigh 3½–4 kg (8–9 lb) at birth and–like the young of most grazing animals—they can see, are well developed and are born with a coat. Within half an hour the lambs have been licked clean by their mothers, and are already on their feet suckling milk from her udder.

Like many baby birds, sheep follow a pattern of imprinting, and ewes will usually accept any lamb as their own if it is given to them a short time after they have given birth. However, after a few hours, a ewe will even reject its own babies if they were removed at birth and others put in their place. Similarly, lambs are very attached to their mothers, and even when they have lambs of their own they will still follow their own mothers wherever they go. This accounts for the expression 'follow like sheep', as lambs will go where their mothers go, who will go where their mothers go, and so on until a whole flock is following the lead of the oldest ewe.

Lambs are born five months after conception, and so rams are normally put among a flock late in the year to produce early spring babies. Most lambs are reared for meat, some for their skins and some for

wool, and the young males are castrated to improve weight-gain. When they are 5–6 months old, lambs of lowland breeds fed on rich grass may weigh around 45 kg (100 lb), and at this stage they normally go to the butchers. Only the best young ewes and perhaps a few young males are kept behind to replace old stock that has been in the flock four or five years.

Piglets: Along with cattle, sheep and poultry, the other most common farmyard animal is the pig. Pigs are kept exclusively for meat, and once upon a time anyone with even a small patch of land would keep a pig for the Christmas table. Nowadays, though, pigs—like everything else—are usually farmed intensively, and special breeds have been developed to produce bacon, ham or pork, with just the right proportions of meat, fat and bone to suit popular human tastes.

Sows and boars both usually become sexually mature at 3–4 months, but they are not used for breeding until 7–8 months. Sows can then produce two litters a year, after a 115-day gestation, becoming fully grown with a weight of 170–250 kg (385–550 lb) at 2–2½ years. Boars of some varieties may reach enormous weights of over 300 kg (650 lb) when they are fully grown, and can be used for mating 200–300 times a year.

Piglets weigh around 1·3 kg (3 lb) at birth, and litters vary in numbers from around 7–14. A few are sometimes killed as the sow rolls on them, cannibalism is not unknown in indoor conditions, and 8–9 surviving piglets is the most usual number. The babies suckle at once from their mother's 12-teated udder, and continue to do so for another 6–12 weeks, during which time they gain weight rapidly. When they are weaned the piglets go on to mineral-rich, cereal-based feed, while the sow is again mated. Pigs mature early, and before they are four months old piglets have reached their prime slaughter weight of 50–65 kg (110–150 lb).

Left: A Syrian Bear mother licks her cubs. Syrian Bears are a different race of the same species as the common Brown Bear, and their normal colouring is grey with a white collar. Fully-grown males may reach an erect height of 2·4 m (8 ft) and weigh as much as 400 kg (900 lb). The cubs, in contrast, are merely lumpy little balls of fur (darker than the adult's) with stumpy legs and an almost non-existent neck. At this stage they are so slight as to bring to mind their near relatives, the dogs, raccoons and weasels. Nonetheless, the cub will grow quickly in the cave den on a diet of its mother's rich milk. Right: This young European Badger cub will, by the time it is two months old, be ready to be weaned. Although it could begin an independent life at this time, it will probably remain with its family in the set until the following spring.

but in winter it moves to lower slopes. As the name suggests, it has black fur—except for a pure white V on its chest and a white chin. It grows to be 1·8 m (6 ft) long, has a pointed snout, small ears and big round eyes. It lives in deciduous forests and is nocturnal, sleeping in a hollow tree or cave during the day and—like other bears—it is omnivorous. Solitary for most of the time, adult males and females come together only to breed. The one or two cubs are born between late January and mid-February and, after they are weaned, they stay with their mother for just over a year.

American Black Bears: Although they once roamed freely through most of the forests of North America, these bears have declined steeply in numbers as human hunters have killed them for meat, fur and trophies. However, those that remain live alone for most of the year, and the sexes only come together in spring to mate. Afterwards they go their separate ways and 7–8 months later—during hibernation—the female produces two or three rat-sized cubs. Until she wakens again in spring the tiny cubs suckle from their mother, and her reserves of fat are enough to sustain them all.

Polar Bears: In complete and not really surprising contrast, Polar Bears—which live on the vast, icy expanses of the Arctic Ocean and its surrounding lands—do not hibernate at all. In fact, swathed in their thick white fur they hardly feel the cold either.

Adult males and females come together during summer to breed, and they stay together until winter begins to set in. Then the male wanders off alone and the female digs a den in the snow, pending the arrival of her babies at the end of the year in mid-winter. The cubs and mother leave the warm den together in spring, and live as a group until the end of summer. The bears spend as much time on the ice-floes as they do on land, stalking and killing seals, young walruses, whale calves and fish. If food is scarce they will feed on carrion or tundra plants. A full-grown Polar Bear may be 3 m (10 ft) tall and weigh up to 750 kg (1650 lb). Despite this great bulk, they are strong swimmers, and swift and agile—being sure- and warm-footed on their big, hairy-soled paws.

Dogs

Wolves and jackals are closely related to domestic and wild dogs, and all belong to the same family (Canidae, numbering some 35 species), as do foxes. However, whereas it is possible for wolves, jackals and dogs to interbreed and produce fertile babies, the fox/dog baby is infertile, and it is extremely difficult to get the two animals to mate at all. With these reservations, and others based on each species' particular environment, the sexual, reproductive and cub-rearing patterns of behaviour of all the Canidae are remarkably similar.

Across the range of the dog family, from wolves at

one end to pet poodles at the other bitches come into season twice a year—in mid-summer and in mid-winter. Normally, litters are of 2–16 pups after a two-month gestation. When the puppies are born their eyes are tightly closed and their bodies, covered in short hair, are shiny and wet. Their mother licks them clean and their coats soon dry to be fluffy and soft. Then the puppies' marvellous sense of smell directs them to the bitch's teats.

For the first few days the puppies stay close to their mother, gaining warmth from her body and strength from her milk which is rich in cream and proteins. They grow quickly and their eyes open at about 10 days. Two or three weeks later they are able to walk, and at one month all their 'milk' teeth have appeared. By this time they look completely different from when they were born. At around six weeks they are ready to be weaned and start on solid food. Their second set of teeth appears at about five months, and by then they are well on the way to self-sufficiency.

Foxes: These are more solitary than most other dogs, except during the late-winter breeding season. Red Foxes are about as big as a medium-sized pet dog, with beautiful red-brown or sandy and white colouring and a bushy, white-tipped tail called a 'brush'. Their long bodies, short legs, long pointed muzzle, big erect ears and elliptical pupils are all indicative of sharp, all-round senses.

One variety which is common to much of Europe and northern Asia is the Old World Red Fox. It generally lives in a burrow, or 'earth', which it has either dug itself, found unoccupied or stolen from another hole-digging animal. In April, 3–8 cubs are born in the earth after a 56-day gestation period. They are blind, but after 7–10 days their eyes open. However, they remain in the earth on a bed of dead leaves and hair until they are nearly a month old, and during this time they suckle from the vixen. When they are strong enough they are taken outside for exercise, and at 10 weeks they are fully weaned and being fed

Left: These Black-backed Jackal pups were born in a nest located deep inside the termite-mound den. They are now playing outside.
Above: A litter of young Coyote pups blend well with the rocky surroundings outside their den.
Right: This Red Fox cub will have been born in an 'earth' prepared and lined by the vixen.

with dead animals. As soon as they are ready the vixen takes them out at night and teaches them to hunt for their staple diet of small rodents, moles, hedgehogs, squirrels and frogs. The cubs finally leave their mother at about six months, and become fully adult when they are a year old.

Foxes are very successful carnivores, who behave similarly in both cities and open country, and only change the details of their secretive lives to adapt to prevailing conditions.

Among the many fox species, the American equivalent of the Old World Red Fox is the American Red Fox, while the Grey Fox is another New World variety. The African Silver Fox is found throughout that continent, and the Pale Sand Fox is found specifically in the Sudan. In the far north there is the Arctic Fox, which changes its coat to a well-camouflaged white in Winter.

Coyotes: These wild dogs, also known as Bush Wolves and Prairie Wolves, are found on the western plains of North America. They are wolf-like, but quite small in size, and bear a resemblance to Australian Dingoes. They are famous for their untiring, loping run, although they can also reach speeds of 55 km/h (34 mph). Like foxes they are nocturnal and during the day they sleep in a burrow, venturing out at night to prey on deer, small mammals and even lambs.

Coyotes live singly, in pairs or in small groups, and their howls are a feature of many films set in the Wild West. The pups are born in a burrow or 'den' after a gestation of 66–70 days, and if—as often happens—they are the result of a cross with a domestic dog, they still retain many Coyote characteristics. At a year old they are adult, and they may then wander

off to meet other Coyotes or stay around with their family. Again, like foxes, Coyotes are adaptable creatures and rely on their keen senses to enable them to live within close proximity of ever-expanding human activity.

Jackals: Although the Common Jackal, like the fox, once inhabited southern Europe in large numbers, by now it has been largely killed off and seeks refuge mainly in the semi-arid wastes of North Africa. By far the most widespread species nowadays is the Oriental Jackal, living right across that continent as far east as Burma. Normally jackals are solitary creatures, but packs often settle themselves in the vicinity of a village or camp, which they enter looking for food and usually disturb with their weird wailing laugh and defensive cackling sounds. However, as jackals like to feed on the remains of kills made by larger beasts of prey, scavenging is a normal activity for them.

The pups are born in a burrow which has been found or dug by their mother. They are blind at first and are suckled for 5–6 weeks. Their development from then on is very similar to foxes and coyotes, and by the time they are two years old they are fully adult.

Domestic Dogs: Dogs and humans have lived together for thousands of years, and the remains of both species have often been found together—sometimes dating right back to Neolithic times. Until a baby dog or bitch is a year old it is known as a puppy, and during this time it quickly learns a range of commands and ways of communicating with its human keepers. Some breeds, of course, have exceptionally sharp senses, intelligence, or a temperament (good or bad, as the case may be) for particular types of work—ranging from 'guard' duties to security patrols, explosives sniffing or farm work. On the other hand, many dogs—kept as 'pets'—owe their comfortable lives to a mutual feeling of companionship between them and their owners.

Whatever the puppy's future, though, the experiences it has during its first few weeks of life are crucially important to its development as a faithful, sociable, well-adjusted adult. Without affection and companionship during these critical weeks—both from its sisters and brothers and much of it from its mother in the form of warmth, milk and reassuring licking—the puppy will not be able to sustain social

well suited to their job. As pups they are warm and affectionate, but they have to be trained with firmness, patience and kindness to cope with their naturally happy, playful personalities.

Unlike hounds, which work mainly with their noses, Sheepdogs use their eyes and ears. Around the world, different types of dogs are used for managing sheep, but the most popular breed is the Border Collie which originated on the English/Scottish border. As a puppy, the Sheepdog's training starts when it is about 12 weeks old. From then on it is taken out every day to get used to the sheep's movements without chasing them round in a 'game'. The puppy then very quickly learns to respond to the calls and whistles of the shepherd. Gradually more commands are learned, until the grown dog is able to manoeuvre whole flocks without ever frightening them into scattering wildly. Such trained puppies can be very valuable, and they sometimes take part in sheepdog 'trials' when they are judged on the style and complexity of their work.

In marked contrast to the lean, speedy physique of the Sheepdog, a fully-grown Swiss St. Bernard may weigh as much as 100 kg (220 lb). At birth, however, this is hard to believe, looking at the hand-sized, blind and deaf puppies. Nonetheless, after only two weeks they can see, and hear a week later. From then on they grow quickly and gradually move on to solid food, so that at three months they are full of energy and ready to start training for their life-saving work of tracking and rescuing people lost in mountains or buried under avalanches. With their keen noses, thick coats and indifference to cold, these dogs excel at their work, and many mountaineers owe their lives to the St. Bernards.

Another big dog seldom kept as a pet is the Husky, which is particularly associated with the frozen North. Although the puppies are weaned after eight weeks, they are left to run free and do not start work hauling sledges until they are over 18 months old and at their full strength. From then on they are tied up for most of the time as they would otherwise fight among themselves and steal any available food.

Finally, in contrast, is the peaceful Labrador, a gun-dog, a popular pet and a steady worker in a wide range of roles. Unlike the free-running young Huskies, Labrador puppies start their training soon after they are weaned and, on police or guide-dog work, they can go on learning for years. Labrador puppies are attractive in their loose-fitting, golden fur coats, and have a gentle, jolly nature.

Above left: Young domestic dog puppies like this Beagle make a pretty picture when they are a few months old. Before then, their eyes and ears are closed and their bodies are rather flabby.
Above right: A pair of Labrador pups sleep peacefully beside their mother.
Right: A Golden Retriever mother patiently feeds her week-old litter.

relationships as it grows older and stronger, graduating at about two months old from a liquid to a solid, meaty diet.

Like all babies, domestic puppies are vulnerable to infections and diseases unless they are dosed with drugs and inoculated by a vet. These illnesses, ranging from simple intestinal worms to fatal distemper, can, however, easily be avoided.

There are so many variations of domesticated dogs, that space only permits a glance at some of the more familiar and famous breeds. Among these is the Beagle, a lovely hound that is popular as a pet in addition to its traditional hunting role in foot-packs with humans in search of small mammals, particularly hares. With their keen noses, and their hound's ability to pick up and follow a scent, Beagles are especially

Australasian babies

Many of the babies born in Australia represent species unknown in the rest of the world. Most of them are reared in their mother's pouches, hatching from eggs either inside, or in rare cases outside, their mothers' bodies. As marsupial mothers do not grow a placenta along with the embryo, the babies cannot be nourished inside her body when they leave their eggs. The tiny, immature embryos have instead to crawl along their mother's fur, making their way into a special pouch. Once there they fix their mouths to a teat which expands to fit, and then they suckle milk until they have developed sufficiently to exist outside the pouch.

Until about 60 million years ago, babies were born and reared in this fashion on every continent. Elsewhere, however, marsupials had to give way as better-adapted, more advanced (placental) animals came along in competition for similar habitats. Australia, though, had by this time separated from Asia and was completely isolated. As a result, the island continent was out of the reach of most placental mammals, and so Australia's marsupials were able to remain unthreatened by new, higher forms of life. Outside Australia, only a very few species of marsupials managed to survive in South America, which was for a long time cut off by a sea from any other land mass.

In 1629, when the first white man (a Dutch sailor named François Pelsart) visited Australia, he thought that the tiny pouched babies he encountered had actually grown from their mothers' teats in the pouch. In 1788, 28 years after Captain Cook had reported his sighting of a kangaroo, white people went to settle in Australia *en masse*, still filled with curiosity at how the mysterious pouched babies were actually born. In 1830 one man—Alexander Collie, a surgeon—saw a kangaroo give birth to her baby. He duly reported all the details, but nobody chose to believe him and the controversy continued until only about 20 years ago when the birth of a kangaroo was finally filmed. With that the mystery was demonstrably solved and the debate at last settled.

Left: Moving freely through the trees with the help of a prehensile tail, this Ringtail Possum carries her baby on her back because it has outgrown her pouch.

Having appreciated in the first instance that the Australian continent was a veritable hot-bed of animals which carried their babies in pouches, people next began to realize that a large number of these marsupial animals looked similar to, ate the same sort of food and lived in the same manner as different placental animals found elsewhere in the world. Gliding possums, for example, were just like flying squirrels except that they reared their young in pouches. Marsupial dormice and Old World dormice were thought to be exactly the same until the babies appeared from the marsupial's pouch, and so on. This phenomenon of totally separate evolutionary processes of adaptation leading to the same, or a very similar, end product is now known as 'convergence'. But the story did not end with convergence. Another interesting realization was that pouched babies, which have almost had the whole of the continent to themselves, have successfully adapted to every type of environment: some as swimmers, others as underground burrowers, one group tree-living, some as runners, others as jumpers and so on. In fact, the marsupials in Australia 'paralleled' placentals around the world in all means of locomotion and every kind of feeding habit to utilize the particular conditions of nature in which each species lived.

Of course not every new baby in Australia is pouched. Baby birds, for instance, hatch from eggs, and include types that will never be able to fly such as Emus and Cassowaries. There are also 109 species of mammal in Australia without pouches, but whose babies grow inside the mother's body in the womb. These include 67 species of rats and mice, numerous bats and also those animals which travelled to Australia with human beings. These include the famous Dingo, which arrived from the north with the Aborigines, and those animals like sheep, cattle, rabbits, foxes, buffalo, pigs, horses, camels and donkeys—many of which now also live wild, having originally been introduced by white settlers.

Finally, there is one further, even more peculiar group of native Australian animals to be considered. These are the monotremes, including the world's only two surviving species of ancient, egg-laying mammals: the Duck-billed Platypus and the Echidna (or Spiny Anteater). These toothless creatures are distinguished as mammals because they are warm-blooded and have many of the essential characteristics such as milk glands and hair. Nonetheless, they are similar to reptiles because there is a single opening for the reproductory and excretory systems, and also because they lay eggs. Curiously the males also have poison spurs on their ankles, which can be used to inject poison into their small victims.

Echidnas: This odd creature looks like a porcupine, but is in fact no relation. It has a long tapering snout, below which there is a small toothless mouth. Its body is covered with short, bristly spines and it has large strong claws which are used to dig into termite nests. Then it uses its long, sticky tongue to collect the insects and larvae, before grinding them against its palate with the horny sections of its tongue and swallowing them when they are crushed.

After a gestation period of about 27 days the female Echidna lays a single egg with a thin leathery shell and plenty of yolk. She deposits this egg straight into a pouch which has developed specially for the purpose, and after about 10 days the baby hatches and is fed

Below: A Woolly Phalanger baby hitches a ride on its mother's back, hanging on with powerful, prehensile claws during a rare sortie out of the dense vegetation.
Right: A kangaroo's pouch can stretch remarkably in size to accommodate her growing baby.

with milk from teatless mammary glands. The milk actually discharges through the surface of the mother's abdomen, and the baby inside the pouch licks it all up. When the baby starts to develop its own spines it is promptly taken out of the pouch by its mother and is put in a safe hiding place among rocks or in a burrow. The mother then visits her baby every other day to suckle it until it is finally weaned at 3–4 months, by which time it is ready to begin its own life. Echidnas are very powerful creatures which can weigh up to $4\frac{1}{2}$ kg (10 lb) and live more than 50 years.

Duck-billed Platypuses: This, the other Australian egg-laying mammal, is a most unusual animal to behold. Rather like an assembly of nature's spare parts, it has a bill resembling a duck's, a body 0·6 m (2 ft) long and covered in fur, and a tail that would do credit to a beaver. At night it feeds in streams on worms and small animals, and during the day it sleeps in a burrow on dry land at the water's edge.

Platypuses mate in water and then the female moves into a special breeding burrow which may penetrate 18 m (20 yd) into the bank, and builds a nest of leaves. She blocks the tunnel behind her, and after about 10 days two eggs are laid. These are soft and white with a leathery skin, and measure about 13 mm ($\frac{1}{2}$ in) in length. The mother sits on her eggs for 10–14 days, then when the babies hatch they are taken head-first into a fold of her skin, as she does not have a pouch. At this stage they are blind, naked, helpless and hardly formed. Baby platypuses suckle in the same way as baby Echidnas, and after about three months their eyes open. Two months later they are weaned, although they stay with their mother for another month before embarking on their own lives.

Possums: The 30–40 species of possum, known collectively as Phalangers, are widespread throughout Australia and (by importation) New Zealand. They are all arboreal creatures with prehensile tails, although some are monkey-like in appearance, others squirrel-like and many small enough to be taken for mice. However, all of them are marsupial, and many— like the Dormouse Possum and the Gliding Possums— show strong convergence with non-marsupial dormice and flying squirrels, for example.

Kangaroos: Australia's best-known marsupials come in three main species—the Grey, the Red and the Euro—which thrive in the semi-arid scrubland that covers much of the continent. A single baby 25 mm (1 in) long is born each year after a gestation of 29·38 days, and it is guided to its mother's pouch by instinct and sense of smell despite being naked, blind and deaf. Using its front paws, which are relatively well developed at this stage, the baby, or 'joey', makes the hazardous climb in about three minutes, and once inside the pouch it promptly grasps one of its mother's four teats in its mouth. Milk is then squirted into its mouth at intervals and the joey grows rapidly for the next 200 days, during which time the pouch stretches to accommodate its burden. By this time the baby is able to leave the pouch occasionally, only to re-enter by gripping the rim with its front feet and sliding in head first, then executing an ungainly somersault to bring its head out in such a position that it can graze along with its mother. During the time the joey is in her pouch, the kangaroo mother is surprisingly unrestricted, and can still take mighty leaps and hop along at speeds up to 48 km/h (30 mph). After about 235 days the young kangaroo leaves the pouch for good, and from then on it takes its place in one of the large family groups to which all kangaroos belong. In the wild, kangaroos appear to live for at least 20 years, and large specimens have been measured at over 2·7 m (9 ft), with a weight of more than 73 kg (160 lb).

Wallabies: The many smaller species of kangaroo, some little larger than rats, are called wallabies. They have smaller rounded ears and when adult, feet that measure less than 25 cm (10 in). Once there were at least 19 different species, but four are now thought to be extinct and another five are very rare. Among the best known surviving species are the beautiful, incredibly agile tree kangaroos and the Quokkas. The Quokka, or Short-tailed Pademelon Wallaby, is a friendly creature which is itself small as an adult, but at birth after 27 days' gestation the baby only weighs a minuscule $\frac{1}{2}$ gramme (about 1/50 oz). Nonetheless, like the kangaroo joey, it is able to climb up into its mother's pouch and there locate a teat. It remains in the pouch for five months, at which time it is ready to start hopping in and out on short excursions. Within another month the young wallaby is completely weaned and will have left the pouch for good. By the time it is 10 months old it will have become completely independent, and at two years it will be a fully adult, breeding member of its group.

Interestingly, but not uniquely among marsupials, wallaby does are able to become pregnant again while they are carrying one baby in their pouch. However, when the fertilized egg has developed into a 100-cell embryo known as a blastocyst, this organism then goes into a sort of suspended animation. If anything happens to the joey already in the pouch, the blastocyst immediately continues its development and a second baby arrives to replace the first one. Otherwise, the 'reserve baby' waits until the joey has permanently vacated the pouch before taking its turn to be born.

Emus: This is a large flightless bird which, along with the kangaroo, features on the Australian coat of arms. The female emu, which is larger than the male, lays 6–20 attractive, dark-green eggs in a flat nest of grass

Right: These three lovely Emu chicks are following father Emu as the males of this impressive, flightless species take over brooding and rearing when their mates have laid the eggs.

Monkeys and apes

Monkeys, Apes and Humans comprise the Sub-order Anthropoids in the Order of mammals known as Primates. There is one other Sub-order of Primates, that of Prosimians, and it includes the Tree-shrews, Lemurs, Aye-ayes, Lorises, Pottos, Bushbabies and Tarsiers. In terms of evolutionary improvement the prosimians (ranging from Tree-shrews up to Tarsiers) are much lower on the ladder than the anthropoids. To further complicate matters, the Monkeys, Apes and Humans are themselves divided into six families which are placed in three groups.

The first of these three major groupings is the New World Monkeys comprising two families: the Marmosets and Cebids. The second is the Old World Monkeys, and all these are placed in one family. The third grouping includes Apes and Humans and is divided into three families: the Gibbons, the Great Apes and the Humans.

Macaques: This is the most common and widespread of the Old World Monkeys; varieties are seen in Asia, the Far East, north Africa and Gibraltar. They are gregarious creatures, recognizable by their thick-set bodies, short, stout limbs and long, rounded muzzles. Some species like the Crab-eating Macaque from south-east Asia have long tails; others, like the Formosan Rock Macaque have medium-length tails, whereas the only two short-tailed Macaques are the Japanese Macaque and the Stump-tail found on the Malay peninsula.

Macaques of all species have very similar habits, and they all live in troops which are often quite large. Each troop is led by an experienced male and is made

Above left: Bushbaby mothers often leave their young in their nest while they are out feeding. There are about three babies in the nest which is made out of leaves and built in the fork of a tree. The babies suckle from their mothers at regular intervals, and from time to time the mother builds another nest for her babies and transfers them from the old nest to the new, carrying them by the scruff of the neck.
Left: In a rocky Ethiopian ravine, a group of female ground-living Gelada Baboons forage for food, one of their number carrying a youngster on her back.
Right: Engrossed in grooming her newly born baby, this Japanese Macaque mother is doing more than just clearing ticks: she is also building a bond of trust and friendship in a way that is common to many animals including humans.

up of females and males of all ages. Under the direction of their leader, macaque troops are expert crop-raiders, spreading out in all directions and immediately stuffing their large check pouches with food to be eaten later at their leisure. The best grains are then sought out and eaten on the spot. Apart from devastating cultivated crops, macaques also eat insects, fruits, seeds and other vegetable matter. They are diurnal and, during the night when dangerous predators roam, they stay well out of sight in the tree-tops.

The single baby is born after a seven-month gestation period and its father may be any one of several males in the troop. When giving birth, the mother macaque suffers very similar stress and discomfort to that experienced by a woman in labour, but her trial is over more quickly. The baby is born head-first, and within an hour its eyes are open and it is able to cling to its mother's fur. It is not a natural climber and has to be taught this skill by its mother. However, it becomes proficient at any height within a year, and by the time it is four and a half years old it is adult and sexually mature. Unless it falls foul of a predator such as a leopard, eagle or snake, the baby will live to the ripe old age of around 26.

Langurs: These slender, luxuriantly-coated monkeys are mainly arboreal and lead peaceful lives in the forests of Borneo, Java, Sumatra, Sri Lanka, India and in Himalayan Tibet. Langurs have a characteristic ridge of eyebrow hairs projecting forward over their faces. Their hands and feet are long and narrow and they are able to move very quickly through the trees. They are also known as Leaf Monkeys as they eat only leaves, shoots, certain kinds of grain and fruit.

Langurs live in large multi-male bands, and groups of Indian Hanuman Langurs are regarded as sacred by Hindus. As is the case with all the primates, breeding goes on continuously among langurs. The mothers give birth to children whose fur is a completely different colour from their own. The females, who take sole parental responsibility for their children, also show a strong interest in all the babies in the group—one will even baby-sit for another while she is out foraging for food. This interest is also nurtured in the juvenile females, and they are encouraged by their elders to handle and play with all the young babies.

Below left: Two baby Leaf Monkeys secure in their parents' arms in the Holy Monkey Forest of Bali.
Below: Baby Orangs weigh only about two kilograms at birth. They travel around clinging tightly to their mothers' fur.

Chimpanzees: These bright, intelligent Great Apes live in the woodland savannahs and tropical rain forests which stretch from Sierra Leone along the west coast of Africa across to the Great Lakes of the Rift Valley. Within this area the one species is divided into several races. Apart from a few white hairs on the chin, an adult Chimpanzee's coat is black or mahogany brown and—unlike other anthropoids— its arms and legs are the same length. Chimpanzees can move very quickly through the trees and when they are on the ground they walk on all fours, although they are able to stand and walk on two feet. They are omnivorous, and their diet includes fruit (particularly bananas), nuts and leaves. They will also eat animals, and they know how to catch termites by poking a stick around in their nests and waiting for them to crawl out along it. Chimpanzees live in families con-

baby's father begins to take a lot more interest in it, and they then play together for the first time.

Young Chimpanzees do not desert their parents once they are old enough to be independent. They stay close by and often help their mother to cope with her next baby. Meanwhile they also play a lot with Chimpanzees of their own age.

At the Institute of Primate Studies in Oklahoma, USA, scientists work with a female Chimpanzee called Washoe. Washoe was adopted by human parents at the age of one, and from then on she was taught a human language: the American Sign Language For The Deaf. By the time she was three she knew more than 30 signs, could use them directly in a wide variety of situations, and also respond to commands. She could even string signs together in simple combinations to ask questions of the humans or tell them what she herself wanted to do. By the time she arrived at the Institute in 1970, she knew over 150 signs and her vocabulary was still increasing. She had even devised ways of combining signs to swear at people who failed to do what she wanted.

Gorillas: Male Gorillas can grow to a formidable 2 m (6½ ft) in height and weigh over 200 kg (440 lb); the females weigh about half as much. They live in the forests and mountains of equatorial Africa, where two sub-species are to be found. The mountain-dwellers are generally larger than the lowland types, and they have a thicker black coat as opposed to the lowland variety's iron-grey colouring. Whatever the sub-species, Gorillas spend much of their time on the ground, where they walk on all fours using their knuckles to support their bodies at a 45° angle with their feet flat on the ground. Although their heaviness prevents many of them from climbing or living in the trees, they spend their days searching for huge quantities of food and eating a varied diet of fruit, bark, bamboo shoots and leaves. Once the food supply in an area is exhausted, Gorillas are forced to move on, and as a result they never have a permanent home. At night they stop and construct nests made of branches and leaves which, depending on the weight of the Gorilla, may be in the trees or on the ground.

Baby Gorillas are small and weak at birth and weigh only 2 kg (about 4½ lb). After their nine-month pregnancy, the mothers have a relatively easy time during labour as, once again, the baby's head is small in relation to its mother's pelvis. Beyond these few details very little is known about baby Gorillas, as adult females and males rarely breed in captivity. However the youngsters grow rapidly, and at about 12 years of age are themselves able to breed.

Above left: Salome, the first baby Gorilla to be born in the London Zoo, has been studied closely since her birth in July 1976.
Right: Orang-utan babies and their mothers form a close bond that lasts long past the time when the child needs its mother purely for physical comfort.

sisting of one or more females, a male, and their children. At night the whole family goes to bed in a nest built in the fork of a tree. They cover themselves with leaves to keep warm and only get up after dawn.

Female Chimpanzees grow to be about 1¼ m (4 ft) tall and the males are usually about 30 cm (1 ft) taller. They become adult between the ages of seven and eight, and are then able to breed. The gestation period lasts for 225 days, and normally labour is easy and short because the baby hardly weighs 2 kg (about 4½ lb) and its head is so tiny. At first the weak little creature has to be supported by its mother as it clings tightly to her belly and suckles. Later, when it is stronger, she carries it around on her back and feeds it whenever it is hungry. However, if the baby Chimpanzee shows any sign of temper or bad humour, it is pointedly ignored by the whole family. After it is weaned the

(350 lb). In spite of their reputation as people-eaters, tigers are only very rarely dangerous to humans, and in fact only 3 in every 1,000 develops a taste for human flesh.

Leopards: This is the most widely distributed of all the Big Cats, being found throughout Asia and Africa. It is smaller than both the lion and the tiger but is nonetheless a fearsome animal with a strong body and long, sharp claws. Each leopard's skin pattern is unique and is made up of closely-spaced rosettes of dark spots against a beautiful tawny-yellow background. The leopard is a good, athletic all-rounder, equally at ease when running, jumping, swimming or tree-climbing. Sometimes it hunts alone, at other times in small groups, but it always hunts during the night as it is a nocturnal animal. During the day it rests well camouflaged in a thicket or cave, or even sleeps in the branches of a tree from where it can drop down on any unsuspecting prey that passes beneath. Often a leopard will use a particular tree as its 'larder', dragging freshly killed carcases high into the branches to be consumed and gnawed over at leisure—well beyond the reach of scavengers.

Leopards, like lions, can breed at any time of the year, and after a gestation period of three months up to six cubs are born in a bush or cave. They are lovingly cared for and suckled by their mother, and they stay with her until they are weaned and strong enough to care for themselves. At first the youngsters hunt for small mammals and birds, but as they mature their experiences lead them to seek larger prey.

Bobcats: The Bay Lynx or, North American Wildcat, which lives in the United States, is recognizable by its reddish-brown, black-spotted fur and black-tufted ears. It grows to over 1 m (3 ft) in length and may be 62 cm (25 in) high to the shoulder. Like all cats, the Bobcat is a carnivore, preying on small mammals, birds and deer. The babies are born during April or May in a well-hidden nest in a den or thicket in the depths of a forest. After a gestation period lasting for three months there are usually between two and four cubs which are blind and helpless at birth. Bobcats' kittens usually stay with their mother for about six months, until they have grown old and strong enough to fend for themselves.

Wild cats: Species of wild cat are found all over the world, except in Australia. They all vary slightly in appearance and choice of habitat, and—most noticeably—some have uniformly-coloured coats whereas others are spotted.

The European Wild Cat and the African Wild Cat are very similar to each other in that they are larger than domestic cats, although interbreeding is still possible. Despite this, the wild cats themselves are fierce animals, afraid of humans and impossible to tame, even as kittens.

The African Wild Cat lives in Syria, India and Africa, and it hunts only during the night. It preys on a very varied range of animals, from antelope to poultry and reptiles, and will also eat fruit and insects.

Although these cats lead solitary lives for most of the year, they do pair up to mate. The kittens are born in a nest prepared by the mother in a den or rocky hollow. The four, blind kittens remain in the nest with their mother who hardly leaves them to feed herself until their eyes are open. Their mother protects them at all times and will fight ferociously in their defence.

The European Wild Cat lives in the forests of northern and eastern Europe, France, Corsica and the Scottish Highlands where there is a sub-species known as the Scottish Wild Cat. This species is a remarkably good climber, and spends the day sleeping high in the branches of a tree where it is well camouflaged and almost impossible to detect. Although it resembles the domestic tabby cat, it is larger and more powerfully built with a much more fearsome set of claws and teeth.

About four babies are born in April or May, and at birth they are tiny, blind and helpless. However they soon settle down to suckling their mother's milk and she stays with them for most of the time, only leaving occasionally to hunt food for herself before returning as soon as she can. Long after they are able to feed themselves, wild cat kittens still suckle milk from their mother, and she cares for them lovingly and plays with them until they are old enough to hunt and lead independent lives.

Domestic cats: The many races of domestic cat are found all over the world, mostly fed by and cared for by humans. Most in Europe are not of any particular specialized breed, but are a mixture of any races which happen to be around during the breeding season. Those cats which live with people soon adapt to the environment, the effortless arrival of food, and their human companions, but they still retain their individuality and independence.

Unless they are 'spayed' and rendered incapable of having kittens, female cats come into season twice a year. At these times they have plenty of tomcat admirers who call incessantly for them. After mating, the female is pregnant for about 56 days and then gives birth to 4–6 kittens, usually in a nest of some sort. As each kitten is born, the mother licks it clean and then encourages it to start suckling. At birth, the babies are blind and helpless with podgy faces and short fur, but their eyes open within 10 days, and by the time they are two weeks old they are starting to take their first unsteady steps. As the weeks go by, the kittens grow rapidly and like true 'copy-cats' begin to imitate their mother's gestures until they are able to wash themselves (and her too).

Right: Research has shown that a kitten separated from its mother at an early age grows up anxious and insecure.

Index

Numbers in italics refer to illustrations

ACKNOWLEDGEMENTS

The publishers would like to thank the following organisations and individuals for their kind permission to reproduce the photographs in this book:

A.F.A. 66 (C. H. Herbert 8); Ardea 7, 42, (V. Collett) 49, (S. Gooders) 90 below, (K. Hog) 57; David Attenborough 90 above; Douglas Baglin 88; Anthony Bannister 51 above; Bavaria Verlag 74–75; Biofotos 44–45; Frank Blackburn 16 above and below; Camera Press 6, 74 above; Bruce Coleman Ltd., contents, 14–15, 23, 27, 29 above, 31, 32, 33, 35, 37, 38 below, 41, 47, 50, 51 below, 52, 54, 58 below, 64, 73, 77, 78 above right, 79, 96, 99, 100; Colour Library International endpapers 19, 20, 63, 68, 92; Anne Cumbers 81 above and below; Donnington Photographics 60; Jacana Agence de Presse 28, 29 below, 43, 62; Paolo Koch 61; Frank Lane 12, 74 below, 97; Claire Leimbach 56; Jane Miller 71; John Moss 101 above; NHPA 21, 30, 34 (M. Morecombe) 13, 82, (I. Polunin) 53; Natural Science Photos 58 above, 78 above left; PAF International 98; Pictor title, 88–89; Pictorial Press 18, 40; Picturepoint 46, 80; John Rigby 22; Bruce Scott 69; Spectrum 24, 65, 101 below; Tony Stone 25, 103; Shin Yoshino 91; Zefa 10, 11, 36, 38 above, 39, 55, 67, 70, 84–85; 87; 93; Zoological Society of London 76, 84, 94, 95;